Family firms

FAMILY FIRMS

STUART ROCK

Published in association with the Institute of Directors

DIRECTOR BOOKS

Published by Director Books,
an imprint of Fitzwilliam Publishing Limited,
Simon & Schuster International Group,
Fitzwilliam House, 32 Trumpington Street,
Cambridge CB2 1QY, England

First published 1991

The views of the author do not necessarily represent those of the
Council of the Institute of Directors.

British Library Cataloguing in Publication Data
Rock, Stuart
  Family firms.
  1. Great Britain. Family firms
  I. Title
  338.7

  ISBN 1–870555–23–6

Designed by Geoff Green
Typeset by The Midlands Book Typesetting Co.
Printed in Great Britain by BPCC Wheatons Ltd, Exeter

Contents

vi   **Contents**

Contents

1 Introduction

The family firm cannot be said to have had a good press over the years. More often than not, they are described as having contributed much to the decline of the industrial and commercial status of the United Kingdom by dint of their having under-invested and by their parochial, inward-looking management style that excluded entrepreneurialism from the boardroom.

Take, for example, Correlli Barnet's assessment in *The Audit of War* (1986) where he analyses the shortcomings of Britain's shipbuilding industry:

For the shipyard owners too continued to be 'practical men' with minimum technical education. The shipbuilding firms passed down in the same families generation by generation; among fifty leading firms in 1914 as many as thirteen still had boards composed solely of members of a single family. In this inward-looking, intellectually incestuous world, the young aspirant to management learned the job by passing time in different branches of the yard . . .

I once asked a Lancastrian textile executive whether the takeovers and closures in the industry were healthy or necessary. 'Oh yes', he replied. As he saw it, it was a cleansing of an Augean stable; there were too many businesses where the money was not being invested in plant, machinery, training or wages but where it was going to pay for the latest toys of the current proprietor. The mill-owner's father may have earned enough so as to afford a villa in Lytham St Annes, but there were even greater things to enjoy with such inherited wealth.

Yet the contribution of family businesses to most Western economies is immense. The extent and range of their control and interests are huge and mysterious. Every country is dominated by them to a greater or lesser extent. But it is only in the United States

1

that a suitably impressive welter of statistics has been gathered over the years.

There are at least 2 million family businesses in the United States with sales of over $1 million. More than 90 per cent of the corporations in the United States are family owned; more than 30 per cent of the Fortune 500 companies are family owned or controlled; 42 per cent of the largest US companies are controlled by one person or family; and family businesses account for more than 60 per cent of the American labour force, for about half of the total wages paid in the United States, and for nearly half of the country's gross national product (GNP). There are those companies where the influence of the family is manifested by voting rights and the company culture rather than through the direct management of the company, as in the chemicals company Du Pont and the motor company Ford. In other instances, they are private reclusive giants such as Mars and Cargill, where the direction and management of the companies remain firmly in the hands of the sons of the founders.

It requires only a cursory look at today's key UK multinational companies to identify those which are still run by families. In the United Kingdom, these include Guinness, Sainsbury, Cadbury Schweppes, Pilkington and Trust Houses Forte (THF). There are also companies such as General Electric Company (GEC) and Maxwell Communications, where it appears that the sons of the chairmen are being groomed for succession. One estimate is that about one-eighth of the FT-100 companies have strong family connections. Some of the most entrepreneurial companies of the 1980s have their roots in a family business, notably the retail jewellers Ratners, the funeral directing business of Howard Hodgson, and the Beazer group of building, construction and materials companies. Then there are the private companies – which include the retail empire of the Moores family, Littlewoods, and the shoe manufacturers in Somerset, Clarks. In the City of London, many of the principal players are eponymous companies – Barings, Rothschild, Robert Fleming.

The situation is the same, if not more so, in continental Europe. Companies of the diversity and size of Bouygues (construction and media), Heineken (brewing) and Henkel (chemicals) are all family owned. Families such as the Quandts hold controlling stakes in BMW; the Porsche and Piech families similarly in Porsche. Massive family disputes have racked prestigious names such as

Gucci and Louis Vuitton Moet Hennessey. One of the largest of Europe's industrial empires – Fiat – is the province of the Agnelli family.

There is little statistical evidence to give a clear picture of the family firm in the overall shape of UK business. The most substantial research – and also the most recent – has been conducted by the London Business School and the accountancy firm Stoy Hayward. A questionnaire was sent to approximately 2,000 private companies and also to companies quoted on the Stock Exchange. It set out to determine quantitatively the success and/or failure factors of family owned businesses, to compare the factors that affected success or failure in owner-managed and non-family owned businesses, and to identify differences between family-run public and private companies. It is an important piece of research, presenting as it does the best representation of the role of the family business.

Stoy Hayward and London Business School listed their findings thus:

Over 76 per cent of UK companies are family owned. The success of those involved in the task of managing family businesses will therefore determine the performance of a substantial proportion of commercial activity in this country. This is a surprisingly high statistic considering the sample consisted of the largest companies in the UK. It seems likely that the actual percentage of UK business being family owned is much higher as the incidence of family ownership amongst smaller businesses would naturally be greater than the UK's largest concerns.

The results of the survey confirm that failure to address promptly the additional management problems facing family businesses affects the companies' future performance and suggest that as companies grow in size it becomes increasingly difficult for them to retain their family status. Family companies remain closely held with 85.5 per cent of such companies having 15 or fewer shareholders, whereas 32 per cent of non-family businesses had 100-plus shareholders. Whilst 7 per cent of non-family businesses had turnover in excess of £200m, only 0.7 per cent of family businesses had turnover at this level.

Overall, non-family businesses achieved a faster rate of growth in turnover, with 39 per cent of non-family companies achieving turnover growth in excess of 20 per cent per annum compared with 25.7 per cent of family companies. Furthermore, whilst 54.3 per cent of family public companies achieved annual growth rate in turnover of over 20 per cent, only 22.1 per cent of private family owned companies reached this level of growth. This confirms the need for family companies to reach consensus on the future of the company and its management practices to sustain the momentum of the business. The family culture can hinder its expansion.

Family companies showed a stronger trend towards long term commitment than their non-family counterparts, with 60.3 per cent of family companies having been established for over 30 years, compared with 34.5 per cent of non-family businesses.

Strategic and succession planning and building the management team are key issues giving rise to substantial differences between family and non-family businesses. Failure to address these issues can cause the business to stagnate. The survey indicated that 40.8 per cent of family businesses are managed by the first generation, 23.9 per cent by the second, and 17.9 per cent by the third. Only 13.7 per cent survive beyond this stage and 3.7 per cent are managed by people totally outside the family.

In a joint study published by Arthur Young (now Ernst & Young) and the Cranfield School of Management entitled *The British Entrepreneur 1988*, an analysis was made of the top 100 owner-managers at that time. The firms they owned, said the report, were not small concerns. The largest had sales of more than £300 million and the smallest more than £15 million. 'Nor', the report added, 'do they fit the stereotype of the old, established, family firm. All except one were founded post-war; the majority are a product of the sixties and seventies.'

One fount for research into family firms is Jordans' table of the Top 4000 privately owned companies. But Jordans admits that the job is a difficult one. 'Medium to large sized private companies are deceptively difficult to research', the company writes. 'The companies are private in the broadest sense of the word – not only in ownership but also in the level of knowledge that is available about them . . . it is still not uncommon for us to learn of "new" private companies for inclusion that have significant turnovers.'

One important piece of research was conducted in early 1989 by 3i Corporate Finance, the advisory arm of the venture capital group 3i. The company surveyed 200 shareholding directors of privately owned British companies with profits of between £250,000 and £5 million and turnover of more than £7.5 million. It was designed to test the attitudes of owners towards selling their businesses.

The survey found that while 37 per cent of those questioned expect to hand down their companies to the next generation of their family, a further third had no plans for any changes in ownership at any time in the future. Seven per cent had no views about the long-term future of their companies.

The attitudes of family owned businesses differed from those that were owned by their management. Almost half (47 per cent) of those interviewed, who defined their companies as 'family owned', planned to hand their company to the next generation of the family. It was the smaller, less profitable, younger companies that were more likely to plan a sale or a flotation. 3i had thought that after ten years of Conservative government, sons and daughters would have been starting up their own businesses. What they found was that tradition was alive and well. One of the questions that was asked was: 'What would make you change your mind about selling?' One-third said that they had no intention under any circumstance unless they ran out of family members. It was, in their view, merely a hypothetical question.

Even with all its contacts and experience, 3i had found itself short of knowledge in a particular market that it serves. It was interested to know what the market was thinking about but could not find previous research on the subject. Further, the company admits to being surprised at the strength of response from family firms. Far from being a fading part of the British business scene, the family business is unquantified, unknown and yet resilient.

So there is an emptiness of true data in this area. There are no textbooks or manuals. This is partly because of the problems of definition. Indeed, for this book I have avoided any specific definition. A family firm can be one where one family holds a majority of the voting shares; it can be one where the family has a cohesive and substantial minority shareholding; it can be a business where the family, by more subtle means, exerts control over its destiny; or it can be a business where a proportion of the senior management posts are held by members of one family and where their children are expected to follow suit. Definition of a family firm is often a case of intuition – one just senses family control in the culture of the company. In the compilation of statistics, the assessment of just what is a family firm is a vague and shifting one. It is also, perhaps, due to a lack of interest. As Stoy Hayward's (1989) report states: 'The words firm and company mean, to most people, large, publicly owned concerns. What automatically springs to mind when we

talk of a family business is a corner shop or a small factory.'
The creation of an enterprise culture in the 1980s has often been
seen to be in opposition to established, inherited businesses;
family firms represent solidity rather than dynamism, caution
rather than risk, and are often antithetical to meritocratic structures.

A bastion of long-termism?

Some people are passionately convinced of this cultural opposition. 'Have British governments discriminated against family
businesses? Yes, yes, yes', asserts Bill Poeton, chairman of a family
owned electroplating business in Gloucester and also chairman
of the Union of Independent Companies, which represents small
private manufacturing firms. 'The Germans saw the importance of
maintaining small family companies as part of their restructuring.
But British governments have not understood the economic role
of the family business; therefore they have not discriminated in
their favour and therefore have prejudiced the sector's ability to
survive.'

On the other hand, many would say that this is not the age
of the family firm. To judge by the findings of the Arthur
Young/Cranfield study and by phenomena such as the growth
of 3i, this is the era of the first generation company. Fifty per
cent of 3i's new investments are either in start-ups or management
buy-outs/buy-ins.

Yet, to paraphrase the nursery rhyme, when family firms are
good they are very, very good – but when they are bad, they are
horrid. It is the horrid stories that have most entertained the Press
and the business journals; it is living soap opera. The qualities that
family firms can bring to the business environment are only now
being appreciated to any extent.

There has been a swelling tide of criticism surrounding the
nature of short-termism in the investment strategies of the City.
It is argued that investors are in for 'the quick kill' or are too
easily enticed by fashion. Perhaps the continuity that can be
afforded by the family business has something to recommend
it.

'We can pursue a path implacably', David Grant once told
me. He is a director of the William Grant whisky company, all

of whose shareholders are members of the family. He can cite Glenfiddich, now the world's biggest selling single malt whisky:

Initially, it was faced with difficulty. People thought that we were lunatic. It was a major investment, as we were distilling ten times more than we were selling, year-on-year for a product that never appeared to be big. Certainly Lord Hanson would never have approved of it!

When the printing firm of W. R. Royle decided that it needed to provide a public relations service to match its annual report writing and production capabilities, it set about building a business from scratch. 'We found an individual and built it around her', says chairman Peter Royle. 'It may be slower but it's the way we wanted it. In this way we integrate the operation so that you obtain true cross-referral of business. It was the same with our design house. The family business is now potentially one of the last bastions of long-term business strategy, with capital regarded as a trust to be passed on and income a reward for performance.'

'You can take the longer-term view', assents Anthony Letts, whose family has been making diaries for several centuries, 'and that's reflected in low staff turnover as much as in commitment to investment.'

'The family ownership gives a business character', reckons William Barker, chairman of the eponymous shoemaking company, 'and I think it rubs off on the day's work. There is happiness here and also a lack of pressure. It's not the end of the road if I have two bad years – I just don't get a dividend! We play a long-term game.' (Barker was able to spend £3 million on a new factory, while turnover stood at around £9 million – a considerable act of faith in the long-term game.)

'I think that family firms will become more attractive rather than less', says Michael Mitchell who, as an "outsider", is chief executive of the family owned store chain of Beales. He continues:

People tend to underestimate the impact on British managers of the mergers and acquisition activity that has gone on over the past ten years. The only one major department store chain that has not been taken over in the eighties has been John Lewis – and that is on account of its protective share structure. This activity destabilises management. Accordingly a lot of retail managers are attracted by shareholder stability.

Seven years ago nobody ever asked me about the shareholder structure when they came for an interview. Now I find that even middle grade managers coming from public companies make it one of their first questions. They are alarmed. Companies have been turned upside-down in unproductive ways by remote people that they have never met and yet who have made an impact on their future.

We offer stability and a diminished likelihood of takeover. We take the boring – or prudent – view of finance. We don't mind borrowing – but never a lot. And we have had six years of steadily growing profits.

Now there are plenty of people to whom this package would not appeal. People who are wanting to take financial risks would not be happy here. We foster a culture of boring, steady, long-term growth.

I have stayed at this company because it is appealing. There are few companies where you have a low risk of takeover, a shareholding not dominated by one particular individual, where all the large shareholders are supportive of a long-term strategy and are not looking for a quick buck. I have room to manage; I have a dozen or so executives who are allowed to get on with it. If we have new ideas we can get on with them. I am not called to account every quarter with dull precision.

'As a family business, you do tend to be fairly safe', acknowledges Michael Passmore, chairman of the Kent-based printing company Passmore International. 'We don't have the same call on available capital, so it makes you cautious about investment decisions. We don't jump in on a hunch but put everything through the rigmarole of planning. You can miss opportunities but our decisions are the right ones nine times out of ten. I remember telling one of our principal – and quoted – competitors that "while he had his eye on his shareholders, we would be picking up orders and doing them because we need just concentrate on our printing business." And he agreed with me!'

Esmond Bulmer, chairman of cider-makers H. P. Bulmer, is not the only person to refer to the bid that was made by BTR for Pilkington. 'I think that debate focused on a world leader that could have fallen into the hands of the financially nimble. If the nimble, with no sense of motivation and no sense of place, win . . . well, you're looking for trouble.'

Bulmer, whose company is publicly quoted but has a protective family shareholding, also refers to one particular rise in excise duties which had a drastic effect on the firm's fortunes. 'It halved our market capitalisation at a stroke.' The share price suffered and, in many circumstances, the company would have been vulnerable to a takeover bid from an acquisitive food and drink manufacturing company. 'If it had not been for family control we would have been taken over', he says.

A congenial and rewarding culture is also identified as a strength of the family firm, as is the commitment of the organisation to its customers and to its products. Service is clearly a forte; otherwise many such small concerns would have folded years ago.

'With a family business you get an overwhelming feeling of paternalism', says Jeremy Moore, who runs Progressive Publicity Group (PPG), an £8 million printing company that was founded by his father (and is now part of the marketing services group Craton Lodge & Knight):

You know the people and you tend to look after them, to have a responsibility. That carries forward. Whatever I want to achieve, I can't, unless everybody else is wanting to do it too. You are reliant on every single individual doing their job to the best of their ability; they are only going to do that if they think that you care for them. Inevitably, frightening things happen with growth. You see someone you don't recognise because somebody else has recruited them. Your initial reaction is to think that things are getting out of control. Then you have to calm down and say to yourself: 'That's what they are there for; that's what they are supposed to be doing.' So you do lose a bit of control but you find yourself always retaining that paternalistic view.

When PPG lost a major contract that amounted to 40 per cent of the overall business, Moore is pleased to point out that not a single redundancy was made. 'It wasn't their fault that the work had gone. They had given everything they could. We took a view to pull in our horns and get on with it, and we did that with everybody's help.'

When George Bateman was faced with a crisis at his family brewery, he stuck to his father's diktat that not a single person should ever be made redundant from Batemans. It stems from when his father laid off a number of workers during the Depression in the 1920s and then took them back on because he could not bear to see them loitering in the streets.

Clive Cutler, who heads Pearce & Cutler, a glass-processing, curtain-walling and glazing group in Birmingham, recalls how increasingly formalised management practices separated the old company culture from the new and which led to the (amicable) departure of his brother. 'The family was no longer hands-on, knowing all the employees, and engaging in all those enjoyable pleasantries. Previously you might have actively sought out the health and welfare of someone but now you might just mention it en passant if you meet the man.'

The importance of having a face that is immediately recognised by the rest of the company is acknowledged. 'With a family business you know who you are working for', says one chairman, 'and this engenders a feeling of confidence. Every employee knows that they are not working for a faceless institution. It also means that communication lines are short.'

Being close to the customer

'Our slogan is that we are a company with a face', says Michael Passmore, 'and that's due to the fact that, as a member of the family, you are always responsible. We may have several faces but we are all Passmores, and as such we are accountable to the shop-floor and to customers. It's a commitment that you cannot shrug off. If customers get upset there is always a Passmore that they can have a go at. I think that the face is a strength.'

At the same time, Passmore admits that it is getting harder for family members to be accepted merely because they are family:

It's not that people are trying to trip you up but that people are going to look at you twice. You are, after all, their future in a sense. It was never easy to prove yourself but it is now certainly harder to make it. However, family involvement does demonstrate continuity; the buck has to stop somewhere. And I think that is preferable to the managing director changing every year.

This perception is held not just by the proprietors of family businesses. Mercedes-Benz UK have run two family business management courses for the sons and daughters of their dealers. Personnel director Peter Padley notes:

In about 1985, there was a great deal of activity in the stock market and our franchise was becoming increasingly attractive. We found that share deals were taking place and we would be informed at a relatively late stage that one of our dealers had changed hands and the business had moved out of a family and into a large group. We felt that this was not necessarily a good thing.

Research we had done showed that possibly up to 30 per cent of our dealer organisation. It could be as high as 40 per cent. While we fully recognised that a professionally run dealership was every bit as good as a family business, we felt – although we couldn't prove it – that there was value in keeping a high content of family businesses in our franchise. We were never challenged on that. We had this impression that, if the owner of the business was on the premises, the chances were that the customer would get a better service. That was the thinnest ice we walked on in presenting the case for a family business course. We have done no research and we probably couldn't prove it, but that's the feeling we have – that there is a direct link. And we kept saying it to those on the course: 'you, as a family business, will probably provide a better service.'

For Caterpillar, the construction equipment manufacturer, distribution depends on a number of family owned and/or managed companies. Studies on behalf of Caterpillar have showed that this relationship was a source of competitive strength. The qualities cited were a commitment to service, the long-term investment perspective, an understanding of the customer and a detailed knowledge of Caterpillar's products and priorities.

(It can, of course, have its disadvantages. Nigel Beale, who is chairman of his family department store, keeps his telephone number ex-directory. Customers have phoned his 75-year-old father at midnight to complain about a fault with their washing machine.)

A long-term vision and a closeness to the customer, allied with pride and knowledge of the product and, in general, short lines of communication and decision – these are the obvious strengths of the family business. (To a whisky distiller like David Grant, being steeped in the production and selling of the product from an early age does give a competitive edge: 'You just have a feel for the product and the market', he says. 'Even a bright manager can miss a point because it wasn't in his formal training book.') But then their weaknesses are equally well advertised. Their access to capital can be limited and the management of succession, if badly handled, can destroy both family and business. Tradition to the point of rigidity can also be seen. And those who are not competent for senior posts can receive them on account of blood alone.

Resolving the financial questions

The financial problems can appear to be intractable, although some would ascribe these difficulties to an unprofessional attitude towards finance.

'I know that some people can run very big organisations quite informally, but my experience – where we were not profitable for some years in the mid-eighties – made us very tight with our money. Just doing that was a major struggle', says Clive Cutler. 'When you have to know at the end of the day what your bank balance is, what it will be the following day, or next week, then you plan. And that requires a hell of a lot of control.' He continues:

This is the problem that a lot of family businesses have been faced with over the years. Unless they have adapted to cash management they have just not survived in the form that they once were. We have had to change our structure to cope with the necessary controls of cash management. That has been the heart of it – constant action plans, controlling capital expenditure. It's quite debilitating when you don't know whether you can pay someone next week because you don't know if you are going to be paid by your supplier.

This has to be at the back of the demise of many family businesses. It's why so many had to sell out. We have survived but the price has been great.

It was a similar story for Jeremy Moore. The business that he entered had provided a comfortable, insulated life. 'It was the wrong environment for thrusting', he says. What prompted him to grow was fear – as the realisation increased that their lack of financial expertise could kill the company:

The business had grown but we were too much in the hands of one client. It was dangerous. So we started to expand but we did not have a financial director – and I couldn't read a balance sheet. We were running rudimentary books. We got more business and we doubled our turnover. It was great fun, exciting and enjoyable, and the family was in it together. But we were not making any money. We were, quite frankly, bloody inefficient. We weren't invoicing people properly.

Any financial sins that might have been committed by the fathers are terribly and surely exacted upon the sons. 'The biggest weakness is that you have to generate your own funds for expansion', says Martin Kenrick, chairman of engineering hardware manufacturers Kenrick and Son. 'In the old days, the family could, within reason, afford not to pay itself. Now, that's just not on. Shortage of cash is a problem. You can't generate enough. Then we also have the burden of some poor investment decisions made some years ago and which have cost us a great deal ever since.'

A flourishing business has emerged among investing institutions, taking stakes in family firms. For many families, it has been the start of the process by which they lose control. So long as the family can see this possibility, these injections of cash are invaluable. Other families regard such institutions with, at best, suspicion and at worst, downright hostility.

'I have thought about such institutions', says one chairman, 'but none of them were interested in us because we couldn't show a profit programme with an exit route for them in the future. We were not in a position to offer ourselves as an opportunity for the venture capital market.'

'I'm biased against them', says one managing director, who has an institution holding a 20 per cent stake in his family firm:

I have an innocuous relationship with them at the moment. They have gained from all my work over the past years and have given me no help at all. There has been no support, not even lending me money at a sensible rate. They are leeches as far as I'm concerned; they are just hoping that I, or someone else, will change our minds and put this business on the USM [Unlisted Securities Market] and they will rake in their profit. I don't even know who 'they' are, because I have watched a faceless stream of young men go in and out of this office and then on to other things.

And, of course, there is still the option to sell. One financial adviser told me of a pair of brothers who thought that they were equipped to take over father's firm but who were palpably not. 'I told the chairman that the best way to ensure his and his family's sanity and his company's future was to put it into a larger umbrella group. Often people come to us looking for money to expand. After discussion, you find that actually they would be quite happy to take on a major role in a large company. Their ambitions can be packaged up into a deal which gives them money, muscle and nothing of the hassle of a flotation.'

2 Putting the business first

If family firms wish to remain independent, the critical point is the transition from one generation to another. There are some other factors which, if managed correctly, contribute towards the smooth day-to-day operation of the firm as well as its long-term success. These typically include a clear and agreed set of objectives, an ability to allow members of the family to find their own level within the organisation and an understanding of family weaknesses as well as strengths. While the dictums of any good management textbook are just as applicable to a family business as to a non-family business, there are perhaps particular aspects of family firm management that are either unusual or which require different sensitivities.

For instance, a family firm has to believe or know that there is a generation that wishes to join the business. Culturally, the feeling that one must join father's firm has been dissipated. There are fewer people who would now reply, as one chairman did when I asked him why he had joined the family firm: 'I never thought of doing anything else, if the truth be known.'

At the same time there appears to be an increase in the number of daughters entering the family business. While it may not be that the sense of obligation is as strong as it was, the pool of potential successors is now wider and deeper. (There are some spectacular examples: the king of soft pornography Paul Raymond has his daughter Debbie in line to succeed him.)

There is a stronger desire to start up a business, to grow it and then to sell it. The concept of the management buy-out, enabling managers and financial institutions to take control of family concerns and offer substantial potential rewards to both parties, is an alluring prospect. Family firms, as much as any other form of organisation, are employing more consultants and outside managers; their influence (as well as the money that they can make) can put a wedge between ownership and management, highlighting the need for formal structures that may be incompatible with the family's desires. The difficulties that surround succession have entertained millions on television – in programmes such as *Dallas* – or in books such as *The Forsyte Saga*. At the core of the longest-running radio programme – *The Archers* – are the interconnected family businesses within the community of Ambridge. Every shift of allegiance nourishes many hours of plot.

The reasons for this seem clear. These problems are ones with which everybody can identify. 'People think of family businesses as having these types of problem because they understand the differences that can exist between their own family group', says one managing director. 'Mother-in-law jokes occur because they are familiar problems. But a family business is no different to any other business in that context. The rows that occur over succession in major public companies are, I suspect, no more or less acrimonious than succession in family companies.' The translation of fiction into normal, understood reality is an easy one. The context may be different; very few of the followers of *Dallas* will own an oil well or a ranch in Texas, but all can understand and assimilate an argument between son and father, or between two siblings.

In dramatising such disputes, the moral standpoint of each character can be clearly depicted. There are those for whom the family is all and who would sacrifice much to maintain cohesion; there are others, usually regarded as the more villainous, who would gladly spurn the wishes of their family to ensure a successful gaining of their way. And there are the uncertain, often the unwitting instigators of a crisis, who endeavour to reconcile their commercial instincts and their preservation of a lifestyle that has been achieved by hard work with a desire for fairness and harmony.

These struggles provide much meat for the scriptwriters. There are endless permutations on the theme: What is fair? What is right? Who deserves what? Do we truly know the extent of the abilities of all parties? Do we know what their framework for decision-making is? (If it comes to the crunch, who will give way?)

The serious difficulties arise when these issues are tested in real life. Although it may seem that the events in *Dallas* are unbelievable, just wait until truth has a go at scriptwriting. The issues that confront the family business are highly complex ones and require remarkable vision and toughness to confront and deal with them

The complexity stems from the blurring between the family and the business, units which are today more usually thought of as being separate units. It is a twilight zone, and in twilight zones collisions can occur. On the one hand is a social unit and on the other is a professional one; in the family firm private life and public life – and the problems of both of them – are interlinked.

Identifying the potential pitfalls

The particular complexities could be summarised as succession, the integration of external management and the correct harnessing of family abilities. The family firms that face these three issues and can say that they emerge from each stage in a stronger condition than before usually prove to be the successful ones.

The crucial ingredient for a smooth succession is communication. If there is ambiguity, or doubt or deferral, there will be problems. Succession depends on all parties understanding why the decision has been made and sticking to an agreed timetable.

How to let go

Letting go is one of the hardest things that the head of a family business can do. One managing director I met had always said that he would retire on his sixty-fifth birthday. When the day came, there was a farewell party. Presents were handed round, speeches were made, champagne was drunk. The next Monday, he was back in the office. There were, he said, some important matters that he hadn't cleared up and that could only be dealt with by him. Weeks later, he was still there, always finding something else to do. The position of managing director had not been filled.

The lines of responsibility and accountability need to be completely clear at all times, but never more so than at the period of transition. If the father, having told the workforce that his son is now in charge, then reacts to the first changes that the son implements by telling the general manager to rearrange things as they were, responsibility has been undermined. The workforce have heard one thing and seen another. The son is not in control; he is still an administrator in the paternal shadow. Many successions do not take place until the father has actually died.

Anthony Poeton was offered the job of group managing director of his father's firm at a time when his father was in his early fifties. Bill, his father, was to become a non-executive chairman. Anthony was surprised but he says that the succession was a smooth one. One of the factors that made it successful was that it was driven from the top, rather than being the result of pressure and frustration from below.

A contract was negotiated; Anthony's personal aims and objectives were discussed. 'He has driven the succession', says Anthony, 'and the credit is due to him. He does not undermine my authority. He gives me room to make mistakes. He gives me confidence to try different ideas. He does not insist on seeing the management papers every week or on knowing how big the overdraft is. He will stand back and talk to me from time to time – and that takes courage.'

Courage is an appropriate word in management succession. Problems arise due to loss of confidence and faith in the younger person's competence. According to Jeremy Moore:

It was a gradual process of my taking on more and more responsibility. He performed the difficult task – standing back and watching me make mistakes without interfering too much. If you don't make mistakes, you don't learn either. It's the best way of learning. In turn, of course, when you are running it, it's difficult to let anyone else do it because you can't sit still and watch somebody do something that you know is wrong.

The need for a plan

There has to be a plan. For a fifth generation family business like Alabaster Passmore, with a number of Passmores involved, it entails plenty of meetings. Five years of discussion preceded their last restructuring of the management chart, determining who should be represented on which board. 'It was clear in our minds and was known internally and to a few customers', says Nigel Passmore, who was promoted from sales and marketing director to managing director, 'but we didn't publicise our deliberations.'

Succession in younger companies hinges on the ability to regenerate a business. The founder of a business can see the possibility of an enterprise outlasting him; he passes the business on to someone who, in all likelihood, is suffering from a degree of midlife *angst*. If there is indecision in the handover; if the founder cannot let go, then the will to succeed can evaporate. 'Many family business problems stem from the fact that they have lost the drive and ambition that initially powered them', says Peter Davis of the Wharton School at the University of Pennsylvania.

Extroverts and introverts

A key element identified by the Stoy Hayward report was that successful family businesses tended to be extrovert in nature. By this was meant that they showed a willingness to change, to collaborate with other firms and to expose members of the family to life outside the family firm. The writers concluded that 'introvert firms which consciously held on to traditional ways, guarded commercial information closely and looked to the family interests first, seemed more prone to problems than the extrovert outward-looking firms.'

What does this mean in reality? It does not necessarily mean any form of corporate public relations activity, as, by their nature, family businesses do not have controlling outside shareholders to whom they must be accountable. Quite a number of family firms that I have spoken to retain a deep suspicion of the Press. Some make a point of 'never speaking to the Press'; others will do so grudgingly.

I wrote once of a company where the boardroom had previously been grandfather's morning room. The managing director could look out across the lawn where he, as a child, had played tennis. It seemed an interesting, illuminating piece of tradition and continuity. Such details were deemed irrelevant by the managing director and he asked for them to be expunged.

Prior to interviewing companies for this book, I sent out a questionnaire for their consideration. Among the questions were ones that asked about disputes within the family:

1. Have family disputes ever threatened the future of the company? Have family members ever left the company?
2. Have family ties ever obstructed boardroom decisions?

The response to such questions offered a fair insight into the extrovert nature of the company. One interviewee told me that I was being 'downright impertinent' to ask such questions. Another said 'yes' to both questions but declined to go further. Others told of long, bruising and intricate stories, involving cousins, brothers, fathers and grandmothers. Those who described such traumas were always clear about the future direction of the company, even if it involved a passing-out of family control. Those who proved more evasive seemed to adopt a more conditional approach to the company's future, or held a complete and unwavering conviction that the next generation would continue to bear the torch.

There is more to this extrovert/introvert vision than the response to a few questions, of course. Other factors include the use of managers from outside the family, the use of outside finance or consultancy, and a greater responsiveness to the market-place.

Employing outsiders

The use of 'outsiders' is, in itself, inevitable. Even those family firms which boast six, seven or eight eponymous directors will employ them. What is important is the extent to which they can carry influence within the organisation. Will they be used as administrators-cum-managers or will they be employed as directors with all that the role entails? Often the promises do not match the reality. In many instances, the most important job that an outsider will hold is that of financial director, if only as a recognition of a lack of trained accountancy skills within the family.

The acid test is whether a family firm could contemplate an outsider being in charge. Very often it is the crucial move in a company's history, and unless managed with skill and firmness it can prove its undoing. A notable instance of where an outsider was appointed to take charge was Guinness, where Ernest Saunders was made managing director. The cultural problems that this can arouse have been described in James Saunders' book *Nightmare* (1989):

Lord Iveagh had been gestating a plan for equal numbers of family members, non-family non-executives and non-family executives on the board, including a significant Irish representation. Ernest, on the other hand, was primarily concerned to recruit competent executive directors to take responsibility for major sections of the business. Ernest: 'As far as non-executives were concerned, I felt that the company needed additional experience from outside the family and from outside Ireland: an American, a European, expertise perhaps from the law, banking and probably from politics.' Iveagh did not disagree, but was nervous about appointing people he did not know. A seat on the board was still considered by the family as a very special honour . . .

And this remains the case for many family firms today – that the board is, if not quite sacrosanct, then at least a sanctum of cloaked genetic prestige. I can recall the shocked look of one chairman when asked whether there were any non-family members on the board. Such a question was regarded as impugning the competence of the family to run their own affairs. On the other hand, the signs are that the trend is towards a far wider mix of interests and people in the family boardroom.

The growing complexity of the business of running a business has been a catalyst. Information technology, increasingly sophisticated marketing and financial methods and a need to manage diversification all put a greater stress on management. The managing director of one family firm (of roughly £20 million turnover and divided into three autonomous units) put it this way: 'To assume that the family has all the abilities to give everything the appropriate management attention would be asking a lot. I have a slightly jaundiced view about the likelihood of family businesses surviving at this sort of level and at this sort of size.'

There are clear problems. Often the family will have no experience of anyone issuing orders; they will only know the fact that they own the company. The family members will be imbued with the culture and the craft of their particular business; if they have all been brought into the business as apprentices and without formal management training, there will be a gap between themselves and the manager who comes from, say, a multinational thick with conventions, classifications and training courses. The family management may be younger than expected or it may be considerably older, causing tensions between the career path of the outsider and the lifetime vision of the family. These different perspectives have to be explored and understood by both parties before the outsider is recruited; if such problems unfold at a later stage, bitterness and politics will take the place of the efficient running of the business.

However, the new generation that is set to take over the reins is more willing to look for advice, consultancy and outside management skills. 'The way family firms are run does reflect a shift in national business culture', says Professor Sue Birley, formerly Philip and Pauline Harris Professor of Entrepreneurship at the

Cranfield School of Management. In her role, she sees this shift evidenced by the number of MBA students who are from family business backgrounds. 'Many at Cranfield – more than you would expect – come from such backgrounds', she says.

Non-executives in the family

Then there is the pressure for a non-executive presence on the board. Bodies such as the Institute of Directors and PRO-NED have been particularly concerned with the promotion of non-executives. It is a message that has not been without its disciples in the family firms. And, while there will no doubt remain many companies whose boards of directors will consist entirely of one name, the outward-looking and independent board will continue to make inroads into the once-private panelled rooms. Says one chairman:

Non-executive directors are important. Being a family business we need outside comment, guidance and contribution. We need someone outside the wood. They will ask questions: 'Why are we doing this?' The family tends to say: 'That's alright, you seem to be doing alright', and just let you go more or less. Nobody tends to jolt you, bring you up. But that needs to be done. We were looking for someone who had been involved in marketing and retail but who also had a strong accountancy background. Certainly we needed someone with experience of high finance in a way that we were not used to, in order to help us with the management of a recent acquisition that we had made.

According to Sir Adrian Cadbury, independent directors can 'be trusted to take an objective view of such questions as family appointments and promotions. The involvement of experienced outsiders in a family firm's decisions is the best insurance against allegations of unfairness in the dealings of members of the family.' He continues, 'A leaven of independent directors will mean that the debates at the board on profit now versus profit in the future, the most difficult of all balances to hold, will be more critical and questioning than if they had been conducted solely by executive board members . . . independent directors also ensure that all directors, whether family or non-family and regardless of seniority, are treated as equal in board meetings.'

Share ownership trends are also changing the cultural horizons of the family business. Although only two British family businesses have so far adopted Employee Share Ownership Plans

(ESOPs), the promoters of such schemes – in which shares are put aside into a discretionary trust for employees as a means of creating a marketability for previously unwanted paper – believe that they will become increasingly popular as a means for garnering together a dispersed shareholding from remote family members.

A reviving interest

Indeed, there is considerable optimism and much constructive thought about the future of family businesses at the moment, provided that the businesses themselves adapt to the circumstances of today rather than believe that because they have survived the competitive environment so far, they will continue to survive into the future.

In the United States, Wharton's Peter Davis points to a whole new field of activity of business study. At least fifty universities offer seminars, courses or special institutes where family business problems can be discussed. 'Scholars', he wrote in the January 1990 issue of *Family Business* (a revealing enough title for a publication), 'are preparing case materials that were until recently in short supply because of the secretive nature of closely held firms. For the first time, a systematic body of knowledge is taking shape that will enable us better to understand the regularities, the unique "laws", governing the normal course of such enterprises.' He continues:

For example, numerous case studies show how firms have drawn up rules that define effective boundaries between family and business, preventing the workings of one from spilling over and interfering with the workings of the other. Yet boundaries do not have to be unbreachable walls. Family values and traditions are the glue that holds a family's business together.

Time and again in my researches I was told of particular problems that, somehow, could only apply to the teller of the story. It was not as if other people did not have problems – and virtually every leader of a family business will, at some stage in the discussion, use the phrase 'clogs to clogs in three generations' – it was simply that the politics, the emotions and the constitutional issues that he or she faced at that time were too private or convoluted or nasty for anyone else to understand. A greater openness, a willingness to discuss – perhaps at seminars for other family firms – might just make people realise that *they are not alone.*

A need for support

Yet in Britain, the infrastructure of support for family firms is absent. Such seminars and discussion groups as are held are usually given an excellent reception. Delegates bare their souls. Managing directors recognise others' dilemmas as their own. Mutual recognition is a great learning tool. The thirst for discussion is apparent; it is up to the firms themselves, as well as advisers, financiers and academics, to promote a climate of openness in which these often difficult issues can be aired.

Sir Adrian Cadbury has called for the establishment of a forum in which this could take place. There is a family firm institute in the United States; there are specialised consultants to family businesses. In Europe, the work is being done at the International Institute for Management Development (IMD) at Lausanne. IMD has also become the centre for a family firm network; perhaps a smaller version of that network should be established in the United Kingdom.

The Mercedes-Benz UK course is an example of what can be done. Volkswagen and Ford in Germany ran similar programmes some years before. It is, perhaps, a reflection of the existing strength of the medium-sized family owned manufacturing sector in West Germany which many, including management guru Peter Drucker, have identified as one of the most significant corner-stones of Western European capitalism in the coming decades. The organiser of Mercedes' courses, Peter Padley, says that 'the most substantive issues came out in group discussion. There was scheduled work which was both stretching and supervised – it was a successful way of transferring business skills. The unscheduled time was more valuable in the sharing of common anxieties, thoughts and hopes. I think that as a result of those sessions, they left being stronger groups than they were before.'

One of the questions that I asked many family firms was about the extent to which they talked to their peers in other such firms. 'Who do you talk to about the business who is outside the business?' There was very little answer. Apart from the necessary chat with the accountant or the lawyer, there was nothing structured.

And yet, given a day or a course wherein to discuss their problems, people are both grateful and enthusiastic for the chance. It is an observation based more on anecdote than on serious research, but it indicates to me that a genuine forum, which could act as a clinic and centre for advice, is required for the long-term prosperity of Britain's family businesses.

What makes an excellent family business?

The definition of an excellent family business is not a universal answer. It depends to a large extent on the size and the objectives of the business. If it is a small, well-established firm that has no desire to grow beyond what is immediately manageable by the family, then the definitions of excellence in management practice will differ greatly from the thrusting first generation business that envisages domestic and international growth.

There are still plenty of questions that can be addressed which will give the family business food for thought. It has to be stressed, though, that as in all management textbooks, nothing written on these pages and no amount of expert advice will ever replace the therapeutic advice of a good scare!

1. Can family members get involved to the degree which they wish rather than to the degree which is wished upon them? Is there a compulsion to join or do family members join because the business is seen to be a desirable company in which to work?
2. Can family members sell all or part of their investment without endangering the independent survival of the business? Would family pressures influence an individual's decisions regarding his or her stake in the company? How flexible are the mechanisms for withdrawal of a stake in the company?
3. Who is represented on the board? Does it represent fairly the executive, the owners and outside interests?
4. Does the salary structure represent fairly the quality of the job being done? Is the decision-making hierarchy based on competence? Do family members report to other family members as necessary? Would you say that all family members within the firm could take orders from a non-family member if so required? Have family members been turned down when they applied for a job in the company?

5. Have family disputes ever threatened the future of the company? Have members of the family ever left the company and why?
6. Have family ties ever obstructed boardroom decisions? How clear is the distinction between private family life and business life?
7. Who controls the destiny of the company and where do the ideas for the future of the company come from?
8. How often is succession discussed, formally or informally? Has a clear successor been decided? Was it a clear-cut decision? Were there others who were suitable? How many people were involved in the decision — and how many of those were not members of the family? If a successor has not been decided, when and how will they be? What would happen if the current head of the firm were to die tomorrow? Has the idea of an outside managing director ever been contemplated?

This is by no means an exhaustive list but the answers to these questions should highlight problem areas. There are some particular personal qualities that need to be applied at all times. The family has to show courage and clarity of vision — the ability to say 'no' even when it might cause short-term hurt. The family has to be honest with itself and recognise its shortcomings. The business has to be flexible, able to change to market circumstances and to personal circumstances. There has to be a commitment, not only to employees, shareholders and customers, but also to professionalism — in many respects, the family business has to be more professionally managed than the non-family business if it is to succeed. And there has to be communication at all times; the subversive network of gossip and hearsay operates, as is well known, in all families.

In other words, the family has to be able to put business first. If this is done, then the careful edifice that combines family and commercial relationships has a chance of stability. There have to be rules and procedures. There has to be clear accountability. There has to be a long-term vision. It may not be how a family operates, but it is how a business has to be run.

3   Solving succession

At the core of any family business lies the issue of succession. If this is not addressed regularly and honestly then no family firm can hope to survive. Many pages have already been written on this subject. It is the basis for the soap opera treatment of the Ewing family in *Dallas*; it is the basis for many academic theses. Yet human beings remain human beings, with an infinite capacity for clouding rationality with emotion and for learning little from the mistakes of others. So the management of succession remains a hardy perennial, intriguing, vexing and often destroying.

The key tenets are always the same. Discuss and plan succession at an early stage and discuss it regularly thereafter. It is only by regular discussion of the issues, both in private and with advisers, that the complexity of the matter is recognised and that an identifiable route through this minefield is signposted. Both parties need to know what is expected of each other and both parties need to have a timetable to which to work. All the options need to be assessed and assessed again; all the possibilities and probabilities need to be built into a succession plan, however unpalatable they may appear at first sight. Realism is all, although the symbolism of succession can often be a great distraction.

The issues that have to be addressed are personal and organisational. The most basic fact that has to be faced is that of death; at some stage, every business owner has to address the prospect of exhaustion, declining powers and, eventually, mortality. It is also a fact that has to be addressed by the children, other relatives and staff. Some may see the facts more clearly and earlier than others but none should be allowed to run away from them.

If the two certain things in life are death and taxes, then family businesses need no reminding that the two tend to travel together.

So succession planning has not just its human face, but its fiscal face as well.

The necessity of order

Order is the key to succession planning. In too many cases, succession has been left to vagary and unpredictability. But it is one of the most certain questions that a family firm has to face. That orderliness can only be assumed if certain questions have been asked:

1. Does the business need to remain family owned, and if so, why?
2. Does the family want to retain ownership, and if so, why?
3. What would happen if the current head of the firm were to die tomorrow? Do you know who would run the firm and what the financial impact would be on it?
4. Is there a consensus among the shareholders and senior managers over the answers to the questions above?

If the answers to any of these are 'don't know' or 'no', then the orderliness that is vital to succession planning is not guaranteed. What succession planning requires is a framework of mutual understanding and clear direction. It is not a subject that can rely on assumption. Having said that, there are some general truths that discussion of succession should bear in mind. The rewards and problems that fall on to a succeeding generation will be substantially different to those that would accrue if the business were to be sold. The training, apprenticeship and impressions that they leave will be a crucial factor for the new generation when they are deciding their future. And succeeding generations want to see the opportunities for both growth and a degree of stability as they contemplate a lifetime of personal and family risk and responsibility.

The mission statement

A mission statement, clearly defining the cultural and ethical aspirations of the family as well as the commercial goals of the company, is an important aid. Such a statement needs regular attention and revision through an audit of both family and non-family management. A company that has a clarity of purpose in its day-to-day work should be able to project that vision forward.

Knowing 'what we are about today' is the first step to knowing 'what we will be about tomorrow'. The mission statement is an integral part of a succession plan. The mission statement is not always easy to put on paper. The energetic founder of a business may have little time for such idle philosophy. The business has been founded on deals, on personal industry, on seizing chances – it has not been built up by grand statements but by sweat of the brow. The founder's ego is, in effect, the mission statement.

It is unlikely that the children of such people are going to be able to formulate a mission statement single-handed. It is, after all, a consensus position in what is probably an autocratic organisation. So the first step is to get the founder to recognise that the time will come when he or she is unable – or perhaps is not the best person – to run the business and that action is needed if the business is to survive them. At that stage, the questions can be asked: what type of company do you think it is now and how would you like to see it develop? What type of company would you like to leave behind? If, as psychologists and students of entrepreneurs tell us, such people regard their businesses as extensions of themselves, as manifestations of their own personalities, then the mission statement has to be in part a recognition of the hopes, fears and limitations of that one personality. Yet it can also help to tease apart the founder's previously interlinked senses of identity and destiny contained within the business. But care has to be taken: for many, discussion about succession is a sign that people are actually hurrying on an untimely end. Indeed, as these discussions should take place when the head of the business is fit and active, embarrassment and discomfiture are less than remote possibilities.

Where the organisation is bigger than this, the mission statement is easier to procure. In turn, succession planning depends less on what one man holds in his locked desk and in his heart and rather more on what the various interested parties hold as important. It is more to do with selecting the right successor, timing it and presenting it correctly, as well as ensuring comfort and security for the outgoing figure.

Deciding on the succession

There are clear options facing a family business at the moment of transition. The business can be sold, either outright or in part to another company or to the employees. A family member can be appointed to take over or an outside, professional manager can take over the helm. If a family member has been earmarked for the job but is considered too inexperienced, then an interim figure can be appointed. In all these instances, the balance between ownership and management has to be kept in focus. How will share ownership, remuneration and executive power be decided in this new phase of the company's history?

The answers to these questions are often enshrined in wills. Yet the will ought not to be the basis of discussion for the ongoing viability of a commercial operation. Separate from a person's will, the answers need to be put in writing and communicated. As with any future corporate plan, it should be the result of intelligent rational discussion. Provided these plans are known soon enough and unambiguously enough, the succeeding generation of family and non-family can plan accordingly.

The issues that confront the management and shareholders of a public company are straightforward. The best candidate is the one who seems most capable of leading the company so as to generate the best return for the shareholders. It is not often that a family will consider the appointment of a new managing director with such clarity. (If they can, then perhaps the sale of the firm is not far off. After all, they are thinking like institutional shareholders, who hold on to their shares for as long as they represent an efficient economic return, rather than as owners of an inheritance.)

The distinction is not, of course, quite as clear as that. Some public companies have become so associated with one person that they adopt a dynastic image almost by chance. Other public companies are associated with one family because of their roots. Their shareholders and their culture may not always be at one.

Usually, the matter of succession is determined by the outgoing chairman/managing director with the advice of non-executive directors or other outsiders. This has been witheringly described by Sir John Harvey-Jones as 'the laying-on of hands system'. The chairman, he argues, has run his or her course by the time of retirement. The temptation will be to recommend or press for a person in his or her own image, or someone that he or she personally favours. So the choice of a new chairman is put into the hands of a trustee at ICI, who acts as a teller for the votes of the directors. (This is a version of the papal secrecy with which, say, the senior partner of a firm of accountants will be chosen.)

While the evidence is that the heads of large public companies tend not to have large personal stakes in the companies that they lead, it is not unknown for the laying-on of hands to be underpinned by a substantial stake in the company. The cases in point are those of Simon Weinstock, who is the biggest shareholder of his father's empire at GEC, or the Kalms brothers who work at Dixons under the stewardship of father Stanley Kalms. One former case was that of Sir John Clark at Plessey: when he took over from his father Sir Allen Clark, he was almost immediately faced with a boardroom revolt. The reason was clear enough: Sir Allen had left his son with only a 3 per cent holding in the business. After that, he established an iron grip on the electronics company without ever actually holding a large stake. (Speculation as to whether Sir John's son, Nigel, would succeed him proved to be premature. Plessey was taken over by the Siemens/GEC joint bid. Sir John did leave an intriguing thought: 'There's a big argument about nepotism and dynasty', he said in one magazine interview. 'Given equal competence, I'd go for family every time.') The other example that dynasty-watchers point to is the presence of Kevin and Ian Maxwell as joint managing directors of Maxwell Communications – with Kevin favoured among observers as the man most likely to succeed when Robert Maxwell finally retires.

For shareholders in these large public companies, there are clear advantages and disadvantages. The nature of family succession spells continuity and stability. It is a reaffirmation of a commitment to manage and to invest. There should be little doubt as to the management's long-term view. Clearly, the dynasties at Sainsbury and Cadbury Schweppes have maintained investor loyalty on those grounds, with proven performance to back them up. This point is also made by Wharton's Peter Davis. His research among US family businesses has shown that among the publicly quoted family concerns, there is a marked ability to outperform the markets. Indeed, a mutual fund called Family Heritage, established as a result of the initial research, outperformed the market considerably.

None the less, there is scope for doubt. Dynastic pride does not necessarily afford the clearest vision. There may well be a suspicion that the only reason the new chairman has been appointed is because of who he is rather than what he can do.

Although it has been reported that about one-eighth of the firms in the FTSE-100 have strong family connections (*Financial*

Weekly, 17–23 November 1989), these are the large exceptions to what is predominantly a small firms rule. The strength and depth of management skills in such organisations should be able to support them even if the supply of kith and kin dries up. Just to prove the point is the example of Pilkington. The current chairman, Anthony Pilkington, is a successor of the original Pilkington brothers who established the glass company. But his predecessor, Sir Alistair Pilkington, was no relation at all – it was merely a happy coincidence that he shared the same name. He was appointed because he was considered the best man for the job, having been the man behind the revolutionary float glass formula that transformed the company. The family, Anthony Pilkington has been known to remark, has been good at kicking out, or not recruiting in the first place, members who were not dedicated to the company. The company's history does seem to show how an effective balance between the needs of the shareholders and the needs of the market-place can be maintained.

The Ford experience

It may be, however, that a publicly quoted family business will return to family leadership after some time under outside management. Many people believe that there will be another Ford in charge of the giant motor company.

The story is an exemplary one – how the largest family business in the world falls prey to the problems that confront the smallest of enterprises. Henry Ford built up the business, being the mastermind of mass production techniques. He also set about destroying the very empire that he had created, in the process humiliating his son Edsel, who had joined the company. In his book The Reckoning (1987), David Halberstam described the events:

By the time he [Edsel] entered manhood, his father was the richest man in the country, unsettled by the material part of his success and ambivalent about the more privileged life to which his son was being introduced. Henry Ford wanted to bestow on his son all possible advantages and to spare him all hardship, but, having done that, he became convinced that Edsel was too soft to deal with the harsh, brutal world of industry . . . He [Edsel] was a capable and confident executive, and an exceptionally well-trained one. His apprenticeship was a full and thorough one – it lasted thirty years . . . it was Edsel's unfortunate duty to represent the future to a father now absolutely locked in a dying past . . . he argued constantly for a new professional managerial staff at Ford; the old man snapped back that if he wanted a job done correctly, he would always pick a man who knew nothing about it. Sometimes he would give Edsel permission to start a project and then, without Edsel's knowing it, gleefully have the project stopped.

The goon squads were used by Henry Ford, and Edsel, among others, was harassed by them. Eventually, it took Ford's wife and Edsel's widow to force the issue of succession. Henry Ford II, Edsel's son, was recalled from navy service (as Halberstam puts it, 'he returned reluctantly, but he was the firstborn of Edsel Ford, and familial obligation demanded it') and was then backed by his mother:

Widowhood had stirred in her the kind of indignation her husband had always lacked. He had been too loyal to challenge his father, but now Edsel's company stock was hers to vote, and she felt a great deal less loyalty. She threatened to sell her stock unless old Henry moved aside in favor of his grandson. Her son would not be destroyed as her husband had been. Clara Bryant Ford backed her completely. They fought off the old man's excuses and his delaying ploys. With that threat, and a sense that these women were intensely serious, Henry Ford finally, furiously, gave up, and Henry Ford II took control.

Not that the second Henry Ford learned anything. Family business management courses had not been invented. He ran the board in autocratic fashion; he lived a colourful personal life by way of compensation for having been dragged into the ugliness of the last days of his grandfather's control. He employed a generation of 'whiz-kids' – firstly, people like Robert McNamara and then Lee Iacocca. The company went public, with the Ford family retaining 40 per cent of the voting stock. Finally, when Henry Ford II died, there was no great sense of family unity. The outside management did not want the next generation of Fords to have a say in the destiny of the company.

Edsel Ford II was, in Halberstam's words, 'making his way far more slowly up the corporate ladder, a ladder that his family no longer entirely controlled'. Academic Peter Davis recalls being asked by Edsel Ford whether he could attend one of Davis' family business courses. Davis was delighted at the prestige such an attendee could bring. There was just one problem: Edsel was denied permission by the human resources manager at Ford. It was a symbol of the loss of control. Now, though, the Ford voting trust has more consensus; it has created a pool of liquidity so that shareholders can get out should they wish and at the same time it has created a stronger voice and influence for the Ford family once more. Many observers would bet that another Ford will enjoy the backing of this trust and that one will therefore see another Ford as chairman within the next twenty years.

The Ford example only goes to show that it is not a question of size of company as far as problems surrounding succession are concerned. For many more family firms, the questions are: when should it take place and how should it be effected?

The transition from the first generation to the second is intrinsically different from that of the second to the third. Transition in larger, more dispersed family firms is different again. Growth, deaths, taxes and external business pressures all play their part in shaping the environment within which succession must take place.

Founders, says Wharton's Peter Davis 'are typically intuitive and emotional people. They obviously have the drive and ambition to build a great business, but they also have a feeling about the place, a love of what they have created that makes them want to perpetuate it through the generations.'

This is both their weakness and their strength. They identify closely with the business, which gives them the commitment to build it. They identify too closely with the business, which makes it difficult for them to let go. The enterprise has reached its current size and shape through their own efforts – so why should anyone else say what is to happen next? Indeed, not only is their competence questioned, so too is their right or even their necessity.

Conquering the founder's reluctance

There are countless stories about monarchical founders. Henry Ford was just one such. 'I'm effectively the financial director for one client', an accountant told me, 'but trying to get the father to relinquish the business was like murder. We only did it when we got him put into a nursing home – and he still won't let go of his shares. He started the company, had it in its good years and now it's suffering badly.'

Then there is the story of the man who founded his business when he was 14. He is now 79 and has only just ceased being chairman and joint managing director. Throughout the 1980s, turnover was flat. Many retailers did not even realise the company was still going. Fossilisation had taken place because the founder had refused to let go.

Harry Levinson describes the process as an attempt to gain immortality:

Each of us in his own unconscious way seeks omnipotence and immortality. To varying degrees, each wants his achievements to stand as an enduring monument to himself; each wants to demonstrate that he was necessary to his organisation, that it cannot do without him. This pressure is particularly strong for entrepreneurs and those who hold their positions for long periods of time. (*Harvard Business Review*, March–April 1971).

The desire to create something that is in one's own image is an eternal human trait. When it intrudes into the field of business, it cuts dangerously across the needs of individuals who work within organisations. It also raises severe tensions between father and children. Will they try to emulate and better him? Will they reject it outright? The children can be brought up in the same controlling manner as the employees are treated at the workplace. Peter Davis describes it as being akin to Louis XIV's axiom: *L'état, c'est moi.*

When this type of control is exerted, succession is almost impossible. In the twilight days of the enterprise, performance of the man and the company will falter. The founder will always want things to be as they were and will repudiate the idea that they can never be returned to that former state. Such hankering can also be seen in the type of founder that Peter Davis describes as the conductor:

They are also very much in control and are central to all decisions in the company . . . They typically invite their children into the business, often enticing them with promises of money, power and prestige. To preserve harmony, they may encourage them to work in different areas of the business . . . they very much enjoy the warmth of family . . . they are able to delegate . . . But . . . as the sons and daughters gain more experience, their personal ambitions begin to intrude on family harmony . . . they are uncertain . . . disturbing questions begin to be asked.

Planning the succession thus presents a huge dilemma that the conductor would prefer to avoid, and usually does avoid for far too long. The frustration of the sons and daughters grows, and they have trouble dealing with it because of their tremendous loyalty to the family and the business.

The compromising element is the notion of fairness. The conductor, as Davis describes the type, wants everybody to be happy.

Happiness depends on his perception that the status quo is operating very nicely, thank you. It is not, therefore, to be disturbed. Questions about the future are deferred or are waved away. This is not because the founder does not recognise the issues; it is because he recognises the threat to order and harmony implicit within those issues. And the chief threat that exists is one of the responsibility of choice. If one of the children is to take over, then others are to be disappointed. The realisation that it is his choice that will cause that disappointment is what holds him back, little thinking that the procrastination is storing up far more problems in the long run.

Not only does this approach lead to frustrated ambitions; it can also lead to financial difficulties. The balanced approach that is required – say, chipping a bit more into the pension scheme, increasing family remuneration – needs to be adopted by all those firms that have a new generation which is to take over the business. But these can be seen as steps that are affecting the future when all the founder wants is to live with the present.

Davis' third type is the technician. These particular types are most often found in businesses that require manual or technical skills – in craft industries, engineering and technology. The founder-technician is brilliant at the job. Administration is delegated.

'Their knowledge and skill is like a magical sword, an Excalibur endowing them with the prestige and power they want.' Either they do not want to pass this knowledge on to their children because that may lead to future usurpation or they are exasperated at the relative slowness that their children show in 'picking the idea up'. As a consequence, the children move away from the business or keep to another area which is separate from father's area of expertise.

Davis concludes that the proprietorial, monarchical types have the greatest difficulty in handing on the business; that conductors have to learn to cope with anxiety while their children have to recognise what their limits will be within the organisation; and the technicians have to learn to form partnerships.

Whatever the type of personality, the basic issue is clear. The founder can be guilty of not discussing succession. The children may often not want to raise the matter, either because of apprehension or because of lack of experience. Yet the issue has to be confronted – and early.

Many founders do not plan succession with any degree of order. Events are usually rather more influential than advice. It is illness or a financial problem that can put an end to the agonising, the waiting and the stagnation. 'Family transitions and company transitions can occur separately and at different times', wrote Barnes and Hershon in the *Harvard Business Review* (1976). 'However, we found that they usually occur together.'

The second and third generations at least have a similar perspective; they both inherited the firm rather than started it. This psychological level playing field means that some of the problems faced by the second generation as they succeeded the founder are no longer there or have been diluted in their significance.

From second to third generation

While the approach to succession from first to second generation is dictated largely by the character of the founder, the transition from second to third generation is much more likely to be dictated by market conditions and by the size and nature of the company. If the second generation has been able to sustain growth and build the enterprise to an appreciable size, the onus on the third generation is to enhance growth while controlling the spreading shareholder interests. If the second generation has elected to keep the business small – or has been unable to grow it – then the onus on the third generation may be to maintain that continuity or to diagnose why growth and development have not occurred, and to find effective remedies. Of course, it has often been the third generation that has sold off the company or has used it as a useful source of cash and thus dissipated its strength.

As the family firm grows and ages, it accretes obligations and interests that were not there at the outset of the enterprise. The small business may have been handed on to two children, each with their own families. This may have led to a widening of the number of shareholders. It may have grown in size, thus increasing the number of employees. It may have had to employ senior management from outside the company. In all these ways, the character and structure of the company are changed. The number of vested interests has grown considerably from the days of the small venture.

Whereas the founder may have had problems in yielding power, the next generations may have even greater problems in apportioning power. There are, after all, rather more options available. The founder and family have grown together. The relationships might have been difficult but at least the issues were straightforward. This is not the case in the following generations, because a single, family-based hierarchical structure cannot just be duplicated and expanded to fit a wider collection of people. If a firm wishes to retain its identity as a family firm it has to maintain relationships within a widening family circle.

Introducing outsiders

Not only does the second generation have to cope with this wider pattern; it will probably also have had to introduce outside managers. Cadbury describes the process of assimilating non-family management as 'one of the hardest issues for family firms to come to terms with'.

Clarity of purpose is all-important. Everybody needs to know just what the plans are for the future of the company and how the transition will be handled. As the company grows, so the interests of family members diverge. This divergence of interests is often used as a convenient excuse by family management not to communicate aims and information, even though it may well be shareholders they are ignoring. The assumption is made that 'they are family' and that, if they are not part of the management of the business, they do not need to know what goes on.

There are other worries. Changing social mores have led to a divorce rate of one in three in the United Kingdom. This has profound implications for passing on the business; the founder, or an inheritor, is mindful that what they bequeath to their children by way of a stake in the company is not such a stable item as it used to be.

'It's very difficult to know how to pass on the shareholding', one chairman told me. He has three sons, all of whom intend to go into the business. He has given them every encouragement to do so. But when I asked about his plans for succession, a cloud appeared on his forehead:

You have to be fair, and all three will get an equal stake. If one then wants to opt out, then it will be up to the other two to buy him out. At least if he doesn't have a part of the business, he has some money out of it. But my worry is marriage. Any one of them could get married and then what happens if there is a divorce? His wife could claim for half.

I have seen it happen to a friend of mine: his father died, his mother remarried a man with two sons, and the business went to those new stepsons. He never saw any part of his father's business. It's a very hard problem.

Another proprietor speaks of the same worries. His son has married a Scandinavian. 'If my son was to die, his wife would be more than happy to take the children and herself back to her home country', he says.

How a successful transition can be achieved

So what is a successful transition? Some would say that it is when family relationships have remained unscathed by the trauma; others might say it is when the business remains unscathed and indeed, strengthened. For most, though, it would be where both sides of the equation remain in harmony.

As far as a business is concerned, the ongoing profitability and stability of the organisation remain paramount objectives at a time of such change. The transition must also herald a new stage of development – whether simply by adapting to meet new market conditions or by the innovation of new products or processes. Change is not necessarily painless – jobs may be lost, for instance – but effective management of change should soften the blows that will fall. In a public company, transition and succession can be like the sloughing off of an old skin or it can mean a change in identity.

Clearly this is not quite the case as far as families are concerned. The sustaining of relationships and of needs is of paramount importance to a family. Problems have to be resolved and threats have to be met and conquered. The death of a father is a different emotional situation to the death of a chairman; to the children working within a family firm, there are two very different demands being placed upon them. One is a commercial pressure: customers still have to be satisfied, a union may still have its pay demand upon the table. The other is far more emotional and focused: it centres on support for the mother and a handful of close relatives and friends.

Yet the management of both are intertwined. The loss of a father can lead to dissension, to old enmities being forced to the surface. It can lead to a loss of sense of purpose, and to emotional and intellectual paralysis. In one survey, it was concluded that eighteen out of thirty such transitions had been unsuccessful (W. Gibb Dyer, *Cultural Change in Family Firms*, 1986, p. 123) and that the businesses had thus suffered.

Putting the right people in place

The family firm must have the right people in place. That sounds simple but it may not be. If a son and heir has been designated chairman-in-waiting, will he have had the appropriate training? If not, what will happen? Who is to oversee the smooth daily running of the business while the period of transition is occurring? Are the appropriate skills in place among other members of staff so as to compensate for the loss of a key individual? Will key customers know what is happening?

These are not questions that can be dealt with at a time of stress and personal loss. They have to be considered beforehand. Ideally, they should be considered at a time when the heir apparent is at the peak of his energetic powers rather than when the 'old man' is in decline:

Although it is quite apparent that a business would be better off making a transition during a halcyon period rather than a turbulent one, many unsuccessful families wait until the crisis occurs before taking any action. Of course, such crises are difficult to predict, but the clear implication for a family business is: if you have a choice and can forecast the future with reasonable accuracy, make the transition when things are going well.(W. Gibb Dyer, 1986, p. 124)

Case study: A. T. Poeton

The example of one particular company – A. T. Poeton – is instructive here. It is a medium-sized electroplating company based in Gloucester. It was founded in 1898 in Bristol, with an early customer being the Douglas motorcycle. Anthony Poeton's great-grandfather built the business and it was passed down the line to his father, Bill Poeton, who took it over in the late 1940s. In 1979 Anthony was made managing director and Bill chairman.

It is in an industry that is well populated with family firms – 'it's a bit of a witchcraft business', says Anthony. 'There are no formalised apprenticeships where you can learn in the practical way what people can learn here being on the job.'

Anthony has two brothers and one sister. One of his brothers works in the firm and is general manager of the operation in Cardiff (in all, there are three companies) and Anthony is adamant that 'he works for me. We are not partners.'

The shareholding is specifically controlled. 'One of the principles that has seen the Poetons through the generations is that there is really one boss, one shareholder', Anthony says. At the moment that is his father, who holds a majority stake. 'I have a reasonable percentage but I don't regard that as mine. As far as I am concerned, my father is the principal shareholder. He owns the company and I am employed under contract to run the business.'

Bill Poeton was effectively chairman until the mid-1980s. He held the post five years after Anthony had held a significant executive position within the company. Now he is not on the board at all; the chairmanship of the holding company is held by Anthony's stepmother. But, as the principal shareholder, he is regularly informed. 'With significant changes, I tend to seek his opinion', says Anthony, 'as I think that it's prudent to make sure that I'm steering the course in a way that my principal shareholder wants me to steer.'

In the meantime, father Bill Poeton has an active campaigning life. His energies – which could still have been channelled into electroplating – are now dedicated to lobbying for private companies and advising on European affairs for small and medium-sized enterprises. His view on succession and control is as firm as his son's:

I was four years younger than my brother but I wasn't prepared to work for him, so I hammered out an agreement that he wouldn't stand in my way. My father made it a limited company in 1954 and I had all the shares. It was quite harmonious but professional advisers played a pretty firm role. My father identified me and I recognised by the same token that my elder son should have it all. It's having the spirit of political trust.

Initially, he had advertised for the post of general manager because he did not think that his son wanted the job. Anthony then expressed an interest if Bill was prepared to step back. And so the agreement was reached. And it was reached before the business wore Bill out and before Anthony was irreconcilably committed to another career.

The need for outside interests

This is another crucial aspect in the planning of succession. The chairman, founder or whoever, has spent many years of his life with the business. It is, to use the cliché, his baby. And it is hard to part with it if all that stretches ahead is a vista of bridge and an uncertain golf handicap. Planning for change means planning not for retirement but for Charles Handy's 'third age'. It entails having other activities, whether it is for the trade association or completely unrelated work. And no one could do that for an outgoing chairman other than the outgoing chairman himself. Successful succession planning is not from the bottom up – it is a top-down process.

Here, too, the role of independent directors or a family council can assist, if only in applying pressure and recommendations on a stubborn leader. It has to be recognised that the man who has made the decisions for, say, the past twenty years is not now going to be told how and when he should finally leave the office. But the consequences of his actions in not relinquishing control and affirming his successor should also be spelled out.

In general, successful change is possible when, like the Poetons, there is a clear understanding of the motives of all parties and of the structure that will replace the old. The outgoing chairman has an interest in the company but has more absorbing interests elsewhere.

Successful change does, of course, depend on whether the successor is competent. It is the appointment of those incompetent to run the company – particularly family members over non-family members – that is the seed of decline. One study in the United States has attributed 45 per cent of all business failures to incompetent new management.

Training new family members

While the subject of training new family members is dealt with in another chapter, it is perhaps salutary to be reminded that this is a perennial problem. In The Sixth Great Power: Barings, 1762–1929 (1988), Philip Ziegler quotes a letter from Francis Baring, written in 1803:

Unremitting attention and exertion through a long life have placed objects within my reach, the value of which are acknowledged by all, but the difficulty to acquire them, and the facility with which they are lost, appear to me to be appreciated by none ... Money or Fortune derive no security from the magnitude or amount, as it cannot be expected that the next in succession will possess equal prudence with the person who acquired ... A man is considered as mean who does not spend his income; and although there are instances of young misers, they are very rare, and the imputation of meanness is so insupportable to a young man, that they never fail to plunge into the opposite extreme. It is for this reason that families founded on the acquirements of an individual do not last above sixty years one with another: families which are founded on the success of public service continue longer, because the Children and Grandchildren of the founder are generally inclined to pursue the same line of Service: but the posterity of a Merchant, Banker etc., particularly when they are young, abandon the pursuit of their predecessor as beneath them, or they follow it by agents without interfering themselves, which is only a more rapid road to ruin.

The voice of the dynasty-builder can be heard. So, too, is the worry that the offspring will not want to follow the father. The northern proverb 'clogs to clogs in three generations' was just as apt then.

As Ziegler points out, another necessity for successful transition is the supply of offspring. Given a plentiful supply, the job of weeding out the good from the bad is made easier:

At any given moment, therefore, there was likely to be a plentiful supply of cousins acquainted with each other and eager for a job in the bank. Elder sons might drop out, deeming the work 'as beneath them', but there were plenty of hungry younger sons who needed to make their fortune. Those at the head of the bank were also ruthless when it came to disposing of the second rate; to carry the name of Baring was not enough, if one could not do the job successfully one was quickly banished to an outpost or consigned to some less exacting line of business. If the right Baring was not there, then somebody was brought in; in ten or twenty years a Baring would no doubt be available to take on the task, but in the meantime it was better that it should be well done by an outsider than bungled by a member of the family. (Ziegler, 1988, pp. 44–5)

This professional view – whose worth is proved by the enduring status of Barings today – has to be matched by a high degree of professional trust between the two generations. There needs to be consensus and a willingness to listen; both parties can and should make a contribution to the success of the business. The father has proved his worth; the son has to prove his.

Anthony Poeton says that the first person to whom he would talk about the business is his father, once he is 'professionally sure that it is sensible'. He adds: 'My father has a long experience of this business and he knows a lot about other businesses. We get on extremely well. I am very fortunate to have a 62-year-old father who gives me advice rather than instruction.'

There are two key phrases in this remark – 'get on extremely well' and 'advice rather than instruction'. The incumbent feels that he is learning from the former chairman; the former chairman is able to pass on ideas and recommendations that involve him in the destiny of the firm and yet which have been asked of him, rather than ones which he feels he has had to force into discussion.

The leader has to train and teach the successor while acknowledging that the successor may well make some mistakes. The leader must also be regularly aware that this is part of the process of letting go, rather than being an isolated form of apprenticeship that will provide him with a capable deputy. The successor has to be able to listen and must show patience. Simple, really, although it's rarely the case in reality.

The problem of fairness

Because the family firm combines the politics and issues of family and business, the management of succession also imposes disciplines on family relationships. Shared views – or at least mutually understood views – are crucial, particularly in the areas of equity distribution, personal and commercial goals and contingency planning. Perceived unfairness in equity issues is what can tear a family apart.

I have heard references among family members working within the company about those family members who are 'merely' shareholders. Parasites, gold-diggers, irritations, ungrateful so-and-so's ... from such a perspective, all they are after is a dividend. It will be these who would sell out if somebody made an offer.

On the other hand, the non-active shareholders find that their role as shareholders – and therefore owners, at least in part – of the company is being ignored. Yet surely they are entitled to their say? Surely they have as much right as anybody within the business? After all, they could have joined.

Within the family firm, there can be tensions. Who is entitled to what? How many shares should be held by whom? Who holds the power? Is everyone being recognised in the most appropriate manner? It may not just be about the basics of ownership (although it usually is), but the criteria upon which the family members debate the future of the company need to be readily understood.

There are any number of philosophical approaches that one can take. Listen to this managing director:

We look at the company as an asset which, if run properly, should produce an income. The running of it is the work. Those that do that work successfully get paid accordingly. If the owner has decided not to sell it and reap all the reward, I don't really understand why the relatives should think it be sold for them to reap the reward. If the owner of the business wants to sell it, then that's his prerogative. He may have chosen not to do that because he wants that business to continue in its current form and because there is a livelihood in it for all the workers. But that business is only as good as it is run. We could run it down and make it worthless. It would only take a few years of bad management and there would be nothing left. My brother and I and the management team are a major part of this firm. It's successful because we have worked hard at this business. That is nothing to do with the shareholders, my cousins or my family. We make the profit, not the shareholders.

Anthony Poeton has a distrust of misplaced fairness. 'The big problem', he says, 'comes when the chap makes no decision about the future of the firm and then divides it up between all the relations'. He continues:

You have then got ten people with 10 per cent each and they have got to come to some sort of agreement with three-quarters of them knowing nothing about the business at all. In that case, you might as well throw the entire thing off the cliff because you will have put an organisation that was in the hands of a dictator into the hands of a committee. That is something we have never ever done. We understand that our business has had one leader – and one owner by and large – all the time. That owner might pick up some moral obligation to other members of the family; that's far better than the other way around where all the members of the family are the owners and have a moral obligation to the managing director. It doesn't really work. Look where lots of people are involved – normally there's a bloody great row. And eventually they have to go public – or lose some of the ownership – in order to pay some distant cousin.

Now, other members of the family can dispute that – but it is a statement of intent. There is little room for the ambiguity and misinterpretation that can dog families if there is any holding back on discussion. Expectations are made clear and the role of the shareholder and the role of the manager are defined.

It is the same when it comes to recruiting family members. Some businesses find it difficult to accept the idea that their children should not want to join the business; others, with equal horror, cannot see why their children should have a job in the company just because it is their father who runs it.

A great many companies are forced into liquidation or sale because of death in the family and the subsequent estate duties. In one recent article in *Forbes* magazine, a tax expert in the United States described the payment of death taxes for family firms as 'like doing a leveraged buyout with Uncle Sam'.

Discussing the unexpected

Rather like making up a will, it is incumbent on everybody to be prepared. Not only should plans be prepared; they should be made known. It is not a subject that others will not think about; it will be discussed behind the father's back. Surely it is more sensible to talk about the plans openly? The unexpected does happen to most people some of the time; pretending to be an ostrich is hardly conducive to the long-term health of the operation. Here, too, the need for non-executive directors and a family council is evident. The non-executive can and should pose these questions. The family council must pose these questions and then determine by consensus what contingency arrangements would be made. In the field of public relations, there is a growing number of specialists who assist companies in practising procedures in order to cope with potential emergencies. Illness or incapacity visited upon the prospective successor of a family business is just as possible as a psychopath poisoning a manufacturer's baby food.

Equally, there should be a designated neutral figure to whom the family can refer at any time of dispute. No matter how well managed, most family businesses will have arguments, even if they are small ones. The structures need to be in place so that a mediator is available.

One suggestion is that family firms have asset management boards. Such a board, it is proposed, would be separated from the board of directors and be composed of key family members who take up issues such as succession planning, distribution of the equity, training and development of family members and so on. Outside consultants or key non-family executives would be brought into this group as and when deemed necessary. This is sensible if there are enough family members to constitute such a board. For many smaller companies, these decisions and the problem-solving may often be for one person. If it is a dispute between generations, it is unlikely that the long-retained solicitor or accountant will be viewed as neutral. The one or two persons should be outside the personal affairs of the family; it is a question of personal judgement as to whether it is better that that person is a hired consultant or a non-executive director with equal responsibility for the future of the firm.

Managing conflict

The ability to foresee and manage possible conflict is one that all family firms must develop. There will be those – the proprietorial founders – for whom this will be difficult. There will be others – whether they be outsiders or uninvolved spouses of family members – who will see it as being merely common sense. No management system is ever going to change such varying perspectives, but regular discussion and open communication can help to bring them closer together.

Particularly with first generation family businesses, this emphasis on discussion and planning is important. The founder, in all likelihood, will have had no experience of anticipating such issues; the second generation, especially if they have not worked outside the firm, will have had no experience of decision-making and will feel trepidation at raising the spectre of possible conflict. That is seen as rocking the boat, undermining authority. The danger is that conflict then has to be decided by a surrogate authority – the law courts. Once a family dispute over the business has to be decided in this way, it is a clear sign that communication has broken down and that the efforts – if efforts there were – to resolve the dispute between the family members have failed. And once the law has been used as a mediator, the effects on family relationships can be shattering. Brother will no longer speak to brother; father cannot bear to see his son. It is far more fundamental than divorce – and the pain with which family firms describe such events should serve as a salutary warning to others.

According to one American student of family businesses:

One of the most powerful forces that can help families make a transition is having superordinate goals that the entire family can agree on and strive to achieve. The tendency in family firms is to do the opposite: to fight for individual self interest rather than explore what might be in the best interest of all parties. (W. Gibb Dyer, 1986, p. 133).

This returns to the need for a mission statement. Once the family has agreed what the aims of the company are – and how those aims integrate with the aims and needs of the family – it can be used as a signpost for the future.

It may be that the greater aims of the family and the company are to preserve the values that were set by the founder. One company that I met had employed a non-family member to run the company for a number of years, despite a long tradition of family ownership and management. The chairman told me that, at the time of making the decision, the family was united in its belief that it was better to have someone who understood the values and the legacy of the company rather than someone who merely bore its name. The succession hurdle was negotiated and, twenty years on, another family member was back in the chairman's office.

On the other hand, the overriding goal might be the maintenance of family control. It may change the shape of the company, but if the will to retain independence is strong enough then it will glue the family together. Or it may be that the shareholders' interests are viewed as paramount. If a family decides to sell, then so be it.

Aesop's fable about the bunch of sticks is used by Peter Davis when holding one of his family business conferences: one stick on its own can be broken with ease; a lot of sticks bound together cannot be broken. The trick for the family business is to find that binding agent. There are no cheap nostrums available.

Communicating with the employees

There is another element. The employees need to know what is occurring. Nothing can be as debilitating for morale and for performance as ignorance and a climate of suspicion and speculation. Within a family business this is more so; each employee has his or her own family, and can relate and compare the politics and the feuding to their own situation. Power struggles in the boardroom may be mysterious; power struggles in the boardroom between siblings or parents and children can be more readily apprehended. Yet at the same time, the family will often attempt to cloak its succession debate in secrecy. The tensions will often tear the company apart.

Succession may cloud the employees' view of the family in a different way. Unless it is clear to all that a successor is to come from the family, there will be the unavoidable charge of nepotism. Industrious and talented management can feel that they are being passed over; shop-floor workers can be cynical about the new head's abilities and interest in them.

The role of the board is important in this area of managing succession, and in particular the non-family and non-executive directors. It is they who can groom – and be seen to groom – the successor. It is they who must communicate to workforce and to customers that a clear plan, based on consensus, is being adopted. It is the board, as well as the family, who must make a public affirmation that it is competence that will rise to the top. But their influence will work only if they have been given the scope by the family in the first place. The family that uses outsiders as tokens will surely be riven by dispute and will make the outsider merely a despairing football to be kicked by rival factions. It is the collective decision of the board to determine the strategy and direction of the company and, when it comes to determining a successor, it should be the votes of the non-family or non-executive director that carry the greatest weight.

How to manage the transition process

The management of succession depends on a great number of factors. It is the nodal point for the development and survival of any family business. It cannot be left as a last-minute issue and it cannot be imagined as necessarily painless. Families need to be mindful of the problems that it has caused many other companies. They need to consult others – whether other family firms or professional consultants – to place their own dilemmas into context.

Firstly, the family business needs to acknowledge the strengths and weaknesses of its current structure. Then it needs to assess its direction, its values and the future pattern of ownership and management. The results of these deliberations need to be communicated clearly to the shareholders, the directors and managers, and to the workforce and the customers. Then the discussion and the planning of succession can start in earnest.

There are some key points for discussion.

1. Structure:
    (a) who runs the company?
    (b) who provides the ideas and who controls the destiny of the company?
    (c) how many people report to the chairman?
    (d) how many of these people are family and how many are non-family?
    (e) what level of decision-making is the leader of the company involved in?
    (f) does the leader of the company involve himself or herself in simple administrative tasks or in those areas for which there is a designated, titular head?
    (g) is the company structure written down on paper or does it emanate from the leader's office?
    (h) who assesses the progress and abilities of those family members who work within the firm?

The answers to these questions should give a clear picture as to how the family integrates with the structure of the company. If it is basically informal – i.e. the ideas come from the chairman's office and there are many different people reporting to the leader directly – then there are structural problems that need to be addressed. It may be assumed that the eldest son will take over, but it is likely that he will not take over until the father's death. As noted above, it is important that succession occurs before this event in order to make the progress of the company comfortable for the customers and the workforce as well as for the family.

2. Direction:
    (a) to what extent are the management goals shared by the rest of the family?
    (b) does the leader prefer to 'run the business him or herself'?
    (c) is the board of directors just a committee?
    (d) do important decisions get discussed by the board or are they just approved?
    (e) what criteria have been employed in the selection and appointment of board directors?

    (f) who wields the influence on the board?

    (g) what is the overall direction of the company? where is it heading?

    (h) what have been the principal changes in size, strategy, use of technology, investment, leadership and use of advisers in the past few years?

Again, one must know on which course the company is sailing and who has put down that course. The notion of a board of directors is to give the company direction; if the direction is being given by hints and signals, or if it is being given by one person, then that needs to be addressed. It may have taken the business on a successful course so far, but is it the right one for the future?

3. Values:

    (a) when and why was the company started?

    (b) what values have informed its history and its actions?

    (c) could it be said that there is a management philosophy?

    (d) if there is such a thing as a management philosophy, how has it been demonstrated?

    (e) how important is the past?

    (f) how are rewards decided?

    (g) which employees – at senior management level – have been particularly successful at their job and why?

    (h) which members of the workforce have been with the company for over ten years?

    (i) are ideas from the workforce ever acted upon?

In this way, some of the values of the company can be established. It may be that the roots are based on a paternalistic and religious view of the world. This will make the culture very different from that of the zealous entrepreneur, who has built a business in order to make a lot of money and who is not overly concerned as to whether his children will take it over or not. The culture of the company is particularly relevant to those family businesses that are considering the use of an outside chief executive or chairman.

4. Ownership/management:

    (a) who owns the business?

    (b) who runs the business?

    (c) how many shareholders are there?

(d) what has been the dividend policy in the past ten years?

(e) how much capital investment and borrowing have taken place over the past ten years?

(f) how many offers have been received by the company?

(g) how have the answers to these offers been decided?

(h) is there a positive or negative attitude towards the sale of all or part of the business?

(i) how many people have voting shares?

(j) how does the salary structure for senior management compare with the standards of that industry?

(k) has employee share ownership been considered?

This is, of course, a thorny problem for many family firms. Once there are members of the family who have a stake in, but not a say in, the business, clear differentiations need to be made; on the one hand there is a reward for running the company, and on the other there is a return for the owners. As the business expands, the succession issue must bear these factors in mind. If the successor is going to spend most of his or her time resolving and tidying issues of dividend and investment, then the older generation is guilty – whether knowingly or not – of a degree of chalice poisoning.

Only once these questions have been addressed can the planning of succession take place. The fortunes of the firm hang on clear lines of communication and an awareness that it is not the only firm to be facing these problems. To treat the issue as a Victorian cleric might treat the matter of sex is hardly the way to propel a business through a critical phase of its life.

Discussing succession openly and honestly

I would suggest a number of considerations to be borne in mind when discussion of succession takes place.

1. It is not the prerogative of the family to determine the outcome. It is a prerequisite that a voice of independence is heard. It would be arrogant to assume that all the necessary skills and insights required to appoint the best possible successor are contained within family members. It would also be odd if all the members of the family could honestly say that there was not some emotion involved in their decision-making. As the Stoy Hayward

report states: 'Good independent advice is the best antidote to the emotional morass that often surrounds a succession.'

2. Succession is inevitable. And, because it is inevitable, it must be discussed regularly as well as early. Wharton School consultant Peter Davis recounts the chief executive who said that his biggest disappointment was not to have had control of the family business by the age of 40. That age is symbolic and must be recognised as such by the older generation – after all, they may have felt that way too.

3. The successor must be well trained. Training and development should not occur solely within the confines of the family business. In that way lies introversion. It was easy when the world of business was smaller; when economies were more tightly knit on a national basis. The British economy cannot be treated in isolation; the future of companies cannot be considered as a parochial matter. Therefore, a more worldly view is necessary. Equally, the opportunities for challenge and travel are far greater; the family business must have an attractiveness beyond that of obligation.

4. It follows, therefore, that the successor must be 'their own man'. If they are put in charge, they cannot be constrained by ghosts of the past. If they are sensible, they will heed advice and will utilise the good name and standing of the company. But they cannot run it in the image of their forebears – and this has to be understood by all who have a stake in the company.

5. It is not going to be easy. Profound emotions are in play. Trust and communication are the keys to making the transition a smooth one.

Understanding the aims of the company

With those considerations in mind there is, equally, an agenda of questions upon which to base discussions. There may well be others, but I believe that this list should stretch most families and outsiders. Some of them I have referred to at the head of the chapter, but they are worth repeating in this context.

1. Does the company need to remain family owned? If so, why?
2. Does the company wish to be family managed? If so, why?
3. What contingency arrangements have been made in case the current leader of the business were to be incapacitated? What

contingency arrangements have been made in case 'the one most likely to succeed' should be incapacitated?

4. What would be the financial impact on the company if the chief shareholder were to die tomorrow?
5. Have the answers to these questions been decided by the family alone?
6. Does the family understand the implications of all the options that the firm could take at the time of transition?
7. Who decides the successor?
8. Who has trained the candidates for succession?
9. What will the retiring head of the company do after his retirement? Will he have a shareholding? Will he have a place on the board? What will be his income?

The attitudes of the successor

There is another aspect of the succession issue and that concerns the attitudes of the successor. It is all very well to be asked to be the successor or to be expected to be the successor, but there are questions that have to be answered. Stewardship of the family business is a privilege for most; but for some it could become a crown of thorns.

This is particularly the case when the prospective successor is working outside of the business. It may be that he or she has thought about a return to the fold but it may also be that such a return has not been envisaged. Stories such as that of Henry and Edsel Ford – or even Vito and Michael Corleone – can sit at the back of successors' minds.

As Sue Birley of the Management School at Imperial College has pointed out, most of the literature on the issue of succession has been written from the perspective of the owner. In 1986, she conducted a survey among business school students at the University of Notre Dame in the United States in order to explore the students' aspirations towards owning a firm of their own. Of the sample of 221, 61 were from family firms.

The students were asked whether they wished to return, would return at some time or whether it was expected of them to return.

Approximately 20 per cent of respondents wanted to return to their family firms within five years; another 38 per cent believed they would return at some unspecified time; and the remaining 42 per cent had absolutely no intention of returning. A very similar pattern of response held for the question about whether students *thought* they would return . . . Over 50 per cent of the respondents claimed that the decision as to whether to join the firm was completely up to them – their parents expected them to join the business only if they wanted to. Another 20 per cent said that their parents didn't expect them to join the firm at all. (*Journal of Small Business Management*, July 1986, p. 40)

Among her other findings, she discovered that not one of the inheritors who intended to return to the business upon graduation or soon thereafter was an eldest child. In other words, the perceived nature of responsibility falling upon the eldest child was a myth.

Another discovery that she made – and perhaps this is not surprising when the sample is from a business school – was that the decision to return to the family business was influenced not just by feelings of responsibility but also by the degree of interest felt in the firm. This interest was expressed not in the nature of the product or the market but in the nature of the strategy of the company. 'Their chief interest was in the firm as an entity – its goals, its direction, its strategy.' (*ibid.*), p. 42)

The family business must present a favourable face to this very demanding public. The older generation may have ways of running the business that will deter the children and must concede that these ways will have to change. It may be particular aspects – such as the appearance of the company logo; or methods – such as the accounting techniques; or styles – does the management eat separately? If the successor is not convinced that he or she can change these, then the succession plan is doomed.

A case study of succession

Take, for example, Michael. He has been working with one of the large management consultancies for several years. He has an MBA. He also has a growing family and he is living apart from them too much for comfort. He is thinking about moving jobs. An offer comes from an unexpected source – his father.

Michael's father's textile operation looks interesting. And Michael and his father get on pretty well. The idea of succession is discussed. And soon Michael realises that there are some fairly major differences between him and his father.

For one, his father keeps everything in his head. He has had decades of running the business and he knows it inside out. He knows where all the managers are; he knows where his fabrics are sold; he knows all the customers and their life stories. He can tell you what is bound where in each of his factories and he can tell you the prices that each roll will fetch. Even where his computer can provide him with the information, he prefers instinct.

Michael, on the other hand, has a classic business graduate's mind. His clients were large companies, employing sophisticated stock control techniques. Retailer relationships were managed electronically through advanced computerised systems which he had helped to implement. He had rarely set foot inside a fabrics store, let alone known any of the managers in one.

But Michael and his father could recognise that they could learn from each other. The salesman could meet the technocrat half-way and they could profit mutually. Michael could not run the business the way his father had – the instincts were just not there. Michael's father reported this to the other family shareholders and to his customers. They understood.

Michael also noticed a lack of direction in the company. This stemmed from the fact that his father had been prepared to let Michael go his own way. The small matter of the eventual destiny of the company was tucked away. For years he had carried the torch. Only now had he questioned himself as to whether he wanted to pass it on and, if so, to whom? Michael kicked himself; he had never bothered to ask his father.

So father had drifted into indulgence. Money was not being reinvested. There had been precious little marketing effort over the past few years but father – and his favoured clients – had enjoyed themselves in the light aeroplane and other foibles of entertainment.

Michael had to insist on father limiting his own income. This was hard. But it meant that Michael had some extra money to invest in the company. Actually, his father had some quite good ideas too, but he had not got around to carrying them out.

And then ownership had to be transferred. Here the experts were brought in. The feisty old man clearly had a lot of life left in him. Michael did not want to have nominal charge; he wanted true authority. For him, it was crucial that he had ownership and that ownership was complete. There were other siblings who did not have Michael's interest in the business and Michael did not want them to have an equal share. At the same time, his father wanted to be able to retire comfortably and did not want to be inequitable in the treatment of his children. The experts devised the appropriate scheme. And it works.

There are still areas of conflict and they are ones that Michael did not foresee in his early discussion with his father. The principal ones are style; Michael's analytical judgement is rather different to that of his father's impulsiveness. And his father has little time or understanding for Michael's wife, who is an important part of the business. To him, women ought not to be in this type of business. It requires Michael to communicate his wife's ideas to him – as he will not listen otherwise.

Understanding different expectations

Michael's experiences are common ones. To make things a success, his father and he had to know each other's expectations. In turn, they communicated these to other relevant parties; in the case of the father, to his customers and to his employees; in Michael's case, to his wife and to those he brought into the operation. Between them, they discussed matters with the rest of the family. For Michael, the biggest lesson has been that all the possibilities have to be discussed beforehand, because the only certainty is that something else will turn up to cause problems once the course of events has been planned.

The older generation has to be aware that even if they enthusiastically welcome their offspring into the organisation, that does not create a debt of gratitude which has to be expressed by the obedient following of corporate rules.

'I hated the idea of company cars', one mother-cum-financial director told me. 'They would be treated as functional items. They would get bashed and nobody would care. I didn't think that people should put any store by them. I failed to see the fillip that the reward of a company car could give to people. I had terrible arguments with my son about this. He wanted me to give a choice of car to the appropriate staff. In the end, I relented, and morale went up. If there is just the one generation in the family business, then you can get stuck in a rut.'

The younger generation will press for changes. Part of the process of transition is the ability to introduce these changes smoothly. The older generation has to introduce elements of change; otherwise there will be too much pressure on the inheritor to do too much all at one time. Yet there must be scope for the inheritor to introduce some things; otherwise their mark will not be made on the firm.

Financial matters are clearly a case in point. Many older proprietors have a reticence about borrowing; the younger generation see borrowing as an opportunity for expansion. Says one proprietor:

Heated arguments between my son and myself always start with budgets. My son has ambitions. I tell him that we haven't got enough money to fulfil them all at the moment. He wants the best in everything while I say that we stick to our existing plans. So we argue. Then we separate and then we talk about it again. I think that when my wife and I fade out he will take on more borrowing than we have ever been prepared to do. We do have a strong little company and we could go for higher gearing. I know that the banks are more reasonable nowadays but I still feel that I want to be in direct touch with the money that funds the business. It's our responsibility and therefore we should be careful. Will our son change this once he is in charge? I must admit to being concerned that he is not cautious enough.

4 Overcoming potential conflict

The stories of strife and acrimony that have riven family firms are legion – as are the reasons behind them. Underlying them all, however, are critical factors: an unwillingness to face the future leading to an inability to change; a misguided sense of fairness that can hide a fatal compromise; and a lack of unity of purpose.

As Bernard Barry (1975) has written, 'family firms face various problems that seem largely to stem from two main sources. One is the confusion of roles that occurs between the social system of the family owning the business and that of the firm itself, and the other is the traditional values that tend to be enshrined by such family enterprises.'

He breaks these problems down into a number of areas. The first is objectives. 'When asked to define their objectives, directors of family firms will usually mention achieving high return on capital employed and fast rate of growth of turnover, but in practice, their behaviour frequently suggests that such aims lie low on their list of priorities.'

Then he suggests investment policy is a vulnerable aspect. In a public company, the shareholders to whom management is accountable will often be faceless. In a family firm, every shareholder and their personal circumstances will be known. 'Management will be very much aware of the needs and expectations of its shareholders and may have to adjust company policy to meet these needs.' He goes on to tell of how an aunt of a managing director consistently refused further investment in order to gain the maximum dividend for herself – which was subsequently channelled to a home for aged horses in the Middle East.

The other key problem area is that of management itself. 'It is in the area of managerial competence that the family firm is probably most subjected to criticism.'

Traditionally, the family firm begins as the creation of one person who combines ownership and management. At that time, it has a unity of purpose. It is an entrepreneurial exercise, requiring single-mindedness and huge amounts of energy. If it succeeds and grows, then it can be put down in the main to the efforts of that one person. The entrepreneur may be lucky; he or she may be succeeded by a son or daughter who is able to sustain the impetus.

Coping with conflicting family interests

But what if the entrepreneur has two or more children? What if only one of them works in the business while the others, equally deserving, have other jobs? What if two of them work in the business? Who is to be given what?

If these represent thorny problems, they become thornier still when faced by a third generation. By that stage, the division between ownership and management has grown wider. It may have reached the point of being unbridgeable. It is one of the basic challenges that faces the management of a family firm to ensure that such gaps either do not occur or that there is a bridge-building programme available.

It tends to be the case that this does not happen until the worst has already taken place. Whether the firm survives after such traumas is usually a matter for the banks, leading to a greater dependence on outside institutions than had ever been previously anticipated or desired.

Take the case of Batemans brewery. The business was started by George Bateman's grandfather, a farmer who rented a mini-brewery with one pub to serve the Lincolnshire agricultural labourers. It developed despite the ravages of rural depopulation, notably becoming the supplier to Billy Butlin's first holiday camp at Skegness. When George Bateman came into the business after the boom years of the Second World War, his father warned him of the struggle ahead. The four Lincolnshire brewers were fighting over the sale of every single barrel. Batemans was the one that survived and gradually built up an estate of nearly 100, predominantly rural, pubs.

The shareholding of the estate was divided between George, his younger brother John and his sister Helen. George and John held

40 per cent each, Helen the remaining 20 per cent. George was managing director while John looked after the wines and spirits division.

The brewery operated an altruistic policy which, if seen as anachronistic by many, earned Batemans considerable respect in the industry and with its tenants. Their father, Harry Bateman, had pledged never to make any redundancies, saying that he would never make a profit out of others' misfortunes. The policy did have a predictable effect on the balance sheet, and through the early 1980s profits and dividends slid.

By the mid-1980s John and Helen had had enough. They announced that they wished to sell their shareholdings. The valuation that they received was higher than George thought he could prudently afford without necessitating a rationalisation of the business. There then followed an acrimonious two-year legal battle. Two completely different attitudes towards the family business were determined through the courts and in the City.

Eventually George obtained a realistic valuation of the business and was able to prove to the Midlands Bank that the company was developing sufficiently to meet the bank charges. A number of pubs have had to be sold. Helen's and John's shares were purchased via an overdraft; Batemans is now owned by George, a family trust and the bank.

'Family companies are very difficult animals', George Bateman philosophises:

I talked to a lot of directors of family businesses and many of them share the same situation; when the company grows to a reasonable size and is in the third or fourth generation you get those with other aspirations rather than continue with the firm that left them that inheritance. My father could only leave shares in the company. He had left a legal framework but it wasn't watertight.

He admits to his innocence of corporate matters. When his brother and sister announced what they wanted to do, he was asked by his advisers whether he had pre-emption rights. 'I replied: "What are pre-emption rights?" I then read all the books that I could find on mergers and acquisitions. I even read a book by Ivan Boesky, the Wall Street insider dealer.'

Now Bateman plans to become a public company. The intention, he says, is that the family maintains control but also that anyone who wants to sell their shares can have a proper market in which to do so. 'The structure has to be big enough in total so that if anyone in the family wants to leave it won't ruin the business', he says. He intends to place the shares with friendly institutions and employee shareholders while it is still in private hands – not forgetting satisfactory pre-emption rights. Getting the balance right is all-important.

Bateman's story illustrates some of the classic problems that can face the family firms. The values of the individual members of the family were in conflict with the traditional values and objectives of the firm. It is often unavoidable, but it can be foreseen. The goals of each member of the family need to be expounded, understood and agreed by everybody. This is particularly the case when some members have a strong executive interest in the company while others have a shareholder/investor role.

The objectives of the business

The relationships within a family firm are determined by a number of factors and they may differ from those within a corporate organisation. Stoy Hayward (1989) describes these differences as ones between 'status, determined by seniority and sentiment' on the one hand, and 'specific skills, knowledge and competence' on the other.

The differences can go further than that and it is vital that they are recognised earlier through mutual discussion. One such difference is that concerning attitudes towards finance.

'Staying the course' describes the non-financial goals thus:

Those firms which explicitly recognise the possible conflict between different objectives and consciously trade off high performance in one area against lower success in another are most likely to achieve over-all success. For this approach to succeed the profit impact of the non-financial goals must be evaluated. Those firms which ignore the existence of goal conflict are less likely to perform well in any area. Too great an overlap invariably leads to an introverted style of management which is disastrous for the firm's commercial success.

The report then cites the following as examples of non-financial objectives in a family firm: building of the family reputation and status within the community; providing employment for the family; providing the store of family wealth; ensuring independence; social goals such as employee welfare; and a dynastic wish to pass on a position in addition to wealth to the next generation.

All of these are fine and worthy motives but all parties must understand precisely how they fit into the mission statement of the company. It would be unwise – even dangerous – to believe that because a company is based upon the family unit it does not need a clear vision of its objectives and the means that it intends to employ to achieve them. In fact, it could be said that the mission statement is of greater importance within the family firm than in the non-family firm.

The need for a creed

The mission statement has been described by others as a family 'creed'. The moral overtones of the word are telling; it tells of a shared belief, verging on the religious, that goes beyond bald corporate objectives. There are few leaders of family firms who go so far as to be mystical in their convictions but many have deep, fundamental passions about their business and its roots. These may not stand square with an objective, adviser-led approach.

None the less, if the 'creed' is treated as a mission statement, collecting and synthesising attitudes and policies on issues relevant to the firm, then the firm can draw strength from it.

The danger, as has been seen above, is when a member, or members, of the family turn against the creed. In effect, they say 'I do not believe.' In Batemans' case, it was a conflict of paternalistic employment and an independent way of life against a need for a secure future investment which could be better achieved by the sale of a shareholding.

Permutations of such a problem are almost endless. More often than not, they result from break-ups within the family. The influence of in-laws, the ramifications of divorce and remarriage, the sudden death of the heir apparent – these are all possibilities that must be written as subclauses into the mission statement. Otherwise, the mission statement will not be robust enough to withstand the shock of changed circumstances.

From dispute to demise

Many examples exist where disputes have resulted in the eventual demise of the company. In the United States they are well documented. The Bingham family in Louisville were owners of a number of significant newspapers, including the Louisville Times. The family feuded so violently that the father elected to sell the company rather than hand it down and leave it to be dismembered by his children. Company founders have passed on shares to their children, only to suffer the indignity of being thrown out and to watch the new generation of shareholders argue in the courts. Forbes magazine cites the instance of Milliken & Co., a textile maker:

After effectively excluding many family members for years from control positions, third generation chief executive Roger Milliken, 73, changed the company's certificate of incorporation so as to lock them out of a say in his succession and prevent the company from ever being sold. The result is a series of bitter lawsuits with possibly more to come.

In most instances, it will be seen that individual desires prove to be stronger than a collective will. They may be stronger because the individual's shareholding in the firm represents a considerable potential asset which they wish to unlock; they may be stronger because the firm itself is a valuable asset over which they wish to gain control. The maximising of power and wealth may be regarded as being more important than the maximising of the business.

Making provision for such attitudes may strike a cynical note but it appears as though too often there is a brushing under the carpet by the incumbent chairman or managing director. It is a 'can't happen to me' approach that is ultimately a short-sighted one.

In a seminal article, 'The family business' (1964), Robert Donnelley wrote:

In a family company, the family almost always has the proprietory and/or management power to pursue its own objectives and aspirations . . . By contrast, the competing interests and values of members of a public corporation check or condition those of the individual (and his family); and the corporate leadership tends to develop, perpetuate and emphasize the institutional values of the firm over those of the individual through formal systems of measurement and incentive . . . In a family enterprise, this organisational enforcement is not native to the system, at least as it applies to family members. The balance between family interests and company interests is usually a psychological one, stemming from the family's own personal sense of responsibility towards the firm.

Using professional advisers

This psychological approach must be made formal. Restraints, objectives, conditions and goals need to be stated and regularly restated. As a charter, a mission statement, it carries the weight of collective agreement. Its details can be determined by close consultation with professional advisers.

The role of the professional adviser is a crucial one. In the United States there are many 'doctors' to family businesses. The most notable of these is Leon Danco, whose Cleveland-based University Services Institute and Centre for Family Businesses has become a training ground for both owners and heirs:

His persistent message is something not all of them want to hear: family business is in trouble and the chief enemy is not the government but themselves. 'He is our shrink', says George Abbott of the National Family Business Council. 'Nobody knows more about the problems of family business.' (Randall Poe, *The Conference Board*, May 1980)

Danco is not the only one. Major business schools have faculties dedicated to the family business. The Wharton School at the University of Pennsylvania has a division for family business studies, headed by Dr Peter Davis. From Massachusetts to South Carolina to Utah, academics and practitioners run courses and seminars for family concerns. Then there is the raft of professional business advice – from accountants, management consultants and the like.

British attitudes to outside guidance

This infrastructure of research, training and courses is not so developed in the United Kingdom. British family firms in need of guidance have limited recourse to advice except that coming from those professionals who already have some stake in the firm, whether it be their accountants or financial backers.

The signs are that this might be changing, although the pent-up demand surely requires a more radical approach. When I asked companies about who they talked to about their business, the answers were often vague or unstructured. Those who talked to other family businesses said that they found it useful, although not directly relevant to their own particular problem. Third party consultants tended to be their accountant and/or their bank manager; while this was seen as a useful way of letting off confidential steam, nobody regarded it as having been of especial advantage – they would talk to their accountant and/or bank manager whether or not they were running a family business. Often, however, the first point of reference was within the family itself. This could lead to the introvert nature of a family business as identified by Stoy Hayward, although that effect is mitigated if the other family member has an extrovert role.

This latter instance is often the case when the father has had the good sense to retire early from executive responsibilities within the firm in order to dedicate himself to outside activities. At this point, the succeeding son has someone to talk to who has a keen interest in what is occurring inside the company but who is distanced from the day-to-day decisions. It does take a strong will on both sides to maintain that distance but it can prove to be remarkably effective. (Of course, the other important part of this equation is the nature of the shareholding; a father with ownership of the company might behave differently to one who has effectively passed ownership down to the next generation.)

Key questions for advisers

So the writing of a clear mission statement can have a binding effect on the family business, and it is an effect that stands outside the psychological and physical ties of the family unit. The adviser who participates in the devising of this statement must be rigorous and impartial with all members. There are some critical questions that the consultant must ask – and answers have to be elicited.

Why is this business still a family business? Too often family members perpetuate a business simply because they were offered a career path that required little effort, or the difficulty of choice. If a daughter or nephew is simply in the firm because 'they had nothing better on offer' or because they thought that 'it was expected of them' then there are clear vulnerable areas within the organisation. Major corporations endeavour to build up a commitment to their organisation so as to retain staff; the same should be said of family firms. The cousin who cannot say why the firm that pays his wages retains the identity of his family is a weakness in the organisation; at worst, that cousin is a potential source of discord as a disloyal shareholder; at best, a drag on the progress of the firm because of a lack of shared commitment.

Are the ambitions and the aspirations of the chairman and managing director known to the rest of the family? This naturally stems from the question above. Family, as well as all the other employees, need to have recognition that they are part of a team working towards a common goal. They will stay with the company if they feel there is continuity and security. That can only come from communication from the top.

And, of course, some of those signals can be misleading. The son who listens to an endless stream of complaints from his father about why the tax system or the unions or the suppliers are no good is hardly being inspired into taking over the reins. Equally, it is very easy for the children not to listen and to ignore just what it is that fires their parents. It may take time to explain, but if these messages are not explained then people act on their own assumptions – and that can be dangerous.

The clarification of assumptions and their conversion into shared aims is at the heart of what a professional adviser can do for a family business. After that, come the hard commercial decisions. Are these goals best achieved by remaining a family business? What abilities do we need and what abilities do we have? While the adviser can advise, these are questions for the family to decide. The adviser must be able to bring them to that point of decision but he or she cannot make the decision for them. It's a case of bringing the horse to water.

The problems that face consultants to family firms are clearly outlined by Robert Metzger (*Journal of Management Consulting*, 1988, vol. 4, no. 4):

The family-controlled enterprise also has unique issues, needs and problems, some of them having to do with size and some having to do with their ownership. Such companies typically have strategic problems with their organisational values, and they often lack a clear mission statement . . .

Family-controlled firms are tough clients. Most consultants, even experienced ones, get caught in two critical contradictions unique to family-controlled firms. The first is the conflict between the pragmatic, here-and-now needs of the firm and the long-range, emotional needs of the family members. The second conflict is between the different overlapping spheres of influence – family members, other owners, managers and employees.

Metzger then proceeds to analyse the problems that consultants face when dealing with family firms. There is an 'emotional reluctance' to discuss the firm's financial situation, as this represents intrusion. Sensitivity also exists over the issue of equity distribution, although it may be over the resolution of such an issue that a consultant is hired in the first place. Questions have to be addressed such as: 'Which generation represents ownership? Which generation represents present or future management? What are the variant needs of each generation? Where are they mutually supportive or in conflict?'

As so often can be the case, it surely is sensible to introduce a consultant at the time when things seem to be going well. A key problem identified by Metzger is that, at the time of crisis, different timescales are employed by consultant and family. The consultant seeks to turn around a business, which often necessitates a sharp paring-down of costs and jobs. The family as a social unit has to be able to survive in the long term and therapists will use patience to resolve family crises. Thus, says Metzger:

Consultants working with troubled family-controlled enterprises must have much greater sensitivity to the longer-term therapeutic approaches necessary to heal family wounds in addition to their predisposition to the short-term tactics used to improve sales, profits, or other measures of performance.

It can and does happen that a family dispute can leave the firm stronger than before. It is a hard way by which to learn improvement.

The Gucci feud

One example of this is Gucci, the Italian luxury goods manufacturer. Cousin fought cousin and father fought son in a variety of lawsuits, although the outcome was seen as having jolted the company's structure into one that was regarded as more responsive to current demands.

What prompted the dispute? In 1922 Guccio Gucci founded the business in Florence. He had three sons, Vasco, Aldo and Rodolfo. Vasco and Aldo entered the business from the start while Rodolfo embarked on a career in films before joining his brothers after the Second World War. The company flourished. (Its current chairman, Maurizio Gucci, has said that his model company is

'Gucci 1960'.) In 1955 Aldo Gucci became chairman. Slowly, the bid for succession among the third generation began.

The most startling event was the ejection of Paolo, one of Aldo's sons, from the company. It was said that he had been challenging his father's authority and demanding a greater say in the running of the business.

Paolo's departure scarcely clarified the situation. Indeed, it made matters worse. The ten years of lawsuits that followed were only to the benefit of the lawyers. Paolo tried to set up his own label and was promptly sued by his father, brothers and cousin. Embittered by this, Paolo then leaked information to the authorities which turned into tax investigations against the rest of his family.

The tax investigations saw the conviction of Aldo Gucci. The chairmanship passed on to his two other sons, Giorgio and Roberto. At this point Maurizio Gucci, the son of Rodolfo, made his claim for outright chairmanship. Rodolfo had left him with a 50 per cent stake in the company and Maurizio was determined to win control via this shareholding.

It was not an easy task. Aldo, Giorgio and Roberto – his uncle and two cousins – alleged that he had forged his father's signature on various documents, including share certificates. While Maurizio was fighting that case, he was also charged with illegal exporting of currency (it has been said that this second set of charges arose from further machinations of his kinsmen).

However, through the use of Bahrain-based Investcorp, other Gucci interests were bought out. By the time that Maurizio had cleared his name (thus allowing him to reclaim his sequestered shares), his cousins were prepared to sell their stake to Investcorp. The financiers held joint control with one member of the family. Investcorp's managing partner, Paul Dimitriuk, said that the new ownership would enable the company to be better managed and allow a clearer strategy to emerge. In the end, no one single person was really to blame. It was a case where all the younger members of the family had their own particular ideas about the destiny of the company. It was a typical third generation split.

Analysts of this particular Italian saga believe that many of the conflicts stemmed from an imperfectly shared vision among the family. Maurizio Gucci has said that everyone was pushing for their own interests. Endless minor variations of the Gucci logo, crest and design appeared on the products, reflecting the differences between the family members. The other manifestation of inter-family problems was the lack of discipline when it came to licensing the name. The Gucci name was cheapened as it was affixed on everything. Now Gucci is cutting back on this widespread practice, revoking many licences; in many of the remaining product areas, the Gucci name is to disappear off the face of the product. Once Gucci has regained its exclusivity, there is a likelihood that Investcorp will oblige the company to go public.

Long-term scenario planning

To many, this particular cycle seems inevitable. 'It has been a tradition for family businesses to wish to survive forever, which is just not tenable', comments David Carter, head of corporate finance at Peat Marwick McLintock. He continues:

By the fifth generation you could have over eighty members of a family. How do you divide rewards between employers and shareholders? Desperate inequalities can arise. There are no certainties of competence in future generations. So the perpetuation of a family business is not necessarily moral. The beauty of a listing is that it brings this problem to a full stop.

The case of Batemans might also prove this point. There had been an assumption that all members of the family were sharing the same aims. This was not the case. After the arguments, after the rancour, the way ahead is seen as being some form of flotation.

But need this necessarily be the case? It could be argued that, as with many other aspects of effective management, if the chairmen and/or managing directors took a realistic view and planned accordingly, then many stories of struggle and strife would at least be diminished in their impact.

There are endless causes for dispute within family firms. They can range from arguments between father and son as to the strategic direction of the company to arguments between siblings for executive control. They can involve disgruntled shareholders without an exit route for their shareholding or disaffected mothers whose sons are not granted the responsibility which they believe their sons deserve.

An important and much-quoted study of these frictions is Harry Levinson's 'Conflicts that plague family businesses' (*Harvard Business Review*, March/April 1971). The first conflict that he identified was the father/son rivalry:

For the founder the business is an instrument, an extension of himself. So he has great difficulty giving up his baby . . . Characteristically, he has great difficulty delegating authority and he also refuses to retire despite repeated promises to do so.

This behaviour has certain implications for father-son relationships. While he consciously wishes to pass his business onto his son and also wants him to attain his place in the sun, unconsciously the father feels that to yield the business would be to lose his masculinity.

At the same time, and also unconsciously, he needs to continue to demonstrate his own competence. That is, he must constantly reassure himself that he alone is competent to make 'his' organisation succeed . . .

The son's feelings of rivalry are a reflection of his father's. The son naturally seeks increasing responsibility commensurate with his growing maturity, and the freedom to act responsibly on his own. But he is frustrated by his father's intrusions, his broken promises of retirement, and his self-aggrandisement.

The son resents being kept in an infantile role . . . He resents, too, remaining dependent on his father for his income level and, as often, for title, office, promotion, and the other usual prerequisites of an executive.

It has to be said that there are many examples where fathers have shown an ability to step aside in favour of their sons (or daughters) with rather less fuss. This tends to happen when the father recognises that he should play the part of chairman while his successor takes over the responsibilities of managing director. This is an area to which I will return.

Sibling rivalry

The second region for dispute that Levinson notes is sibling rivalry:

Their competition may be exacerbated by the father if he tries to play the sons off against each other or has decided that one should wear his mantle . . . In my experience, the greatest difficulties of this kind occur where there are only two brothers in the organisation.

The problem is further complicated if their mother or their wives are also directly or indirectly involved in the business . . . The rivalry between brothers for their father's approval, which began in childhood, continues into adult life. It can reach such an intensity that it colours every management decision and magnifies the jockeying for power that goes on in all organisations.

From this stems the third key problem area – other relatives. 'In some families', writes Levinson, 'it is expected that all those who wish to join the company will have places there. This can have devastating effects, particularly if the jobs are sinecures.'

'It was just like *Dallas*', one chief executive of a medium-sized public company told me. 'A group of us were meeting in one restaurant, discussing how to rid ourselves of various aunts and uncles who were voting against my proposals. The aunts and uncles were meeting just up the road to discuss how to get rid of me.'

If a family business is run autocratically or monarchically, the oldest brother will become the managing director or chairman and his siblings will be allocated roles on the basis of order of birth. Ability can take a back seat. Similar inequities can occur if a brother-in-law enters the business and proves to be better than his newly acquired peers.

Anticipating problems

Up to a point, these problems are inevitable. But only up to a point. How can they be anticipated and discussed before matters blow up into a crisis?

I have said that many disputes occur by either an unwillingness to face the future, a misguided sense of fairness that breeds compromise, or a lack of unity of purpose. To confront these issues, what is required is toughness, openness and regular self-assessment.

When boiled down to its essentials, facing the future means planning for succession. This can be hard, particularly for a founder of a business. There is the most brutal of questions: what happens if the current head of the firm is run over by a bus tomorrow? Who will replace them? Will that choice be made by all members of the family? Is it likely to meet with general approval – by shareholders, managers and employees?

Openness means a frank and honest understanding as to how the company is run. There is even less room than in a non-family organisation for saying one thing and delivering another. While many family managers are driven by a sense of duty and some can thrive on that, it is clear that many are promised responsibility but are not granted it. It is incumbent upon those who run the family business to train and prepare their successors – not as they themselves were trained but as modern managers are trained. Merely learning the trade in which the business is involved is not going to lead to effective future management. At the same time, the new generation have to be given a clear picture as to how and when they should be promoted to the next level of responsibility, depending upon performance. (I would suggest that such assessment and analysis of performance be conducted by the most senior non-family member of the company.)

The mission statement, combined with a shared knowledge of succession and of how the business is structured and operated, should go some way to giving the unity of purpose that every company needs.

The family audit

These issues could be discussed at a regular family audit. This would bring together all members of the family actively involved in the business plus leading shareholders (if their stake was deemed substantial). Such a meeting need only be held once or twice a year and could be chaired by an outside consultant. Then matters of progression, development and corporate aims would be discussed. Such a system would be particularly useful for those companies where more than one strand of the family is represented within the firm. Naturally, these matters will be discussed over breakfast and dinner tables anyway, but their formalisation could act as a reasonable guide to the way the company is adapting to change as well as providing a better framework of reference than most hazy recollections of conversations. It would also act in addition to, rather than as a replacement of, performance appraisals conducted during the year.

There are key areas that need to be discussed, if not at each meeting then certainly regularly. These are the family's views on the distribution of the equity, on the management of contingencies, and on goals and lines of responsibility.

The family's view of what is 'fair' and 'equitable' is often the one factor underpinning many of the problems experienced during a transition period. If family members feel that they are not receiving their fair share, they often attempt to undermine the efforts of others ... difference in stock or assets are a function of some criteria – experience, expertise, commitment – that family members recognise as valid ... Determining what criteria are relevant, how to measure them, and how to resolve disagreements are often serious problems, but somehow the successful family firm manages to make those determinations. (W. Gibb Dyer, 1986, p. 131)

Planning for contingencies should always be on the agenda, particularly if the market in which the firm operates is a fluid one. It is much the same situation as when a personal will may be redrawn based on changes in one's personal life. And, like many people's attitudes towards wills, there is an element of 'it couldn't happen to me'. Within this contingency arrangement must lie the anticipation of a power struggle or conflict, particularly when the chairman has been a strong one. Here, too, the necessity of training for the new generation as well as clear and open discussion are the least likely to have been practised; yet they are the most important for survival.

If the family firm has a public mission statement, then the goals of the company should not be a problem. Circumstances may, of course, change them slightly. The lines of responsibility ought to be understood, based as they are on day-to-day executive practice. However, it is clear that attempts will be made to influence management decision-making at an informal, kitchen table level. This in itself is unavoidable, but the two types of discussion must be disentangled as far as possible. The politically motivated weekend chat must never carry as much executive weight as the decision thrashed out in the boardroom. If a regular family meeting clarifies the correct lines of decision-making, then the influence of the informal discussion will be understood by all and less emphasis will be put upon it by those who believe that it may be a way of short-circuiting the sometimes undesirable, but correct, reporting to a non-family executive. Equally, it will show the non-family executives that the family is determined to run the company as a company rather than as a way of providing jobs for relatives.

5 Sharing and selling

A number of important changes occurred in the corporate environment during the 1980s which have given family businesses a greater degree of choice over their destiny. It is now possible for employees to become shareholders and yet not to feel tied by that ownership of shares. The development of the Unlisted Securities Market has enabled many family businesses to float off a portion of their shares without ceding control and yet giving them access to the capital markets. There has been a proliferation in the number of venture capital and development capital companies. At the same time, there has been a small but significant trend towards private ownership; a number of British companies have delisted themselves from the stock market and many other private firms have decided not to seek a public listing. So the choices facing a family firm are perhaps more complex than ever before.

Tax considerations

At the same time, the tax regime has changed. The burden of death duties and estate tax has been lessened over the past years. This, plus the lowering of income tax, has greatly favoured the continuation of family ownership rather than promoting the sale of enterprises. While this chapter will outline the options that a family business faces, it is in no way a substitute for professional advice.

It is, of course, never too early to start the planning process. There have to be contingency plans to guard against unforeseen tragedies. What is required is that the family has its objectives clear so that its advisers can work from certainties rather than from confusing and often different signals.

The principal question that must be answered in the tax planning stage is whether there is to be a family successor. If there is not, then it is more likely that a sale of the company will occur – a step which requires timing and preparation. If, however, a transfer of power to the management team is contemplated, then a series of gradual and tax-efficient steps will have to be made. Provision needs to be made for shareholders to be bought out on an equitable basis if, say, shares have passed on to those deemed unacceptable in the future running of the business.

It is clear that owners of family businesses who plan ahead can make considerable tax savings when the business is to be sold or passed on. As with the issue of management succession, it is most advisable to take action at a time of growth and stability. Tax, like corporate strategy, has to be considered on a long-term basis.

Taxation: the political context

There is also the political context in which the taxation regime works. The Conservative government has reduced income tax to the same level as capital gains tax and inheritance tax. This means that inheritors are better off than they have been for some time.

The reasons for this are part of the government's political philosophy. In announcing the reductions in inheritance tax (IHT), the then Chancellor Nigel Lawson argued that they favoured enterprise.

This is a debate that has a long and political pedigree. There are those who argue that inheritance is intrinsically wrong and that it has perpetuated inequalities in the social system. The inheritors of a business are not always likely to have the same entrepreneurial zeal as their parents. In this respect, critics cite the Bolton Report on small firms which said:

We are not convinced that the economy necessarily benefits from the retention of control of a business inside a single family ... it should not be assumed that the children of a successful entrepreneur will necessarily inherit his acumen and energy. Certainly we should not equate a change in management with the extinction of the firm.

Critics of the lowering of inheritance tax also point out that there are many entrepreneurs who either do not have children or who do not have the intention of passing the business on. Yet, as entrepreneurs, they continue to build their business. In other words, the incentive of lower inheritance tax is not really an incentive at all.

Indeed, the free market argument is turned around. The death of the person who founded and drove a business should be the opportunity for placing it on the market. The highest bidder would then put it to its most efficient use, rather than hoping that a successor will 'do something with it'. In a way, it tests the market philosophy to its logical extent. Others believe that nobody should be free from the necessity of work (and this includes certain proprietors of family businesses), while yet others maintain that all should have an equal start in life. For example, there is the case of Warren Buffet, the American investor whose personal wealth is estimated at $1.5 billion. Buffet, it is said, intends to leave his children with 'only' a few hundred thousand dollars. He has been quoted as saying that it would be antisocial to set up his children 'with a lifetime of food stamps just because they came out of the right womb'. (the *Financial Times*, 22 February 1990)

The fiscal policies pursued by the government, it is argued, have contributed to a widening of the gap between rich and poor. On the other hand, it is argued that inheritance is a necessary creator of wealth, provided that it remains in private hands. Inheritance tax, therefore, is destructive in that it attacks the source of potential further wealth creation.

It has been argued, furthermore, that the entire concept of IHT on family owned, private companies should be abolished outright. In a research monograph for the Institute of Economic Affairs (1989), Barry Bracewell-Milnes outlines the proposal.

He points to research on the profit and growth rates of quoted and unquoted companies between 1966 and 1979 which showed that the unquoted sector performed considerably better. Bracewell-Milnes then argues that ownership commits the owner-managers to long-term measures and long-term success and that owners of established family businesses regard themselves more as trustees than as outright owner-managers. He writes:

Quoted and unquoted companies (and unincorporated family businesses) have their respective strengths and weaknesses. They should be allowed to compete on level terms. This is not possible as long as inheritance tax is levied on the shares of unquoted companies and other assets of unquoted businesses. In order to secure equality of tax treatment between quoted and unquoted businesses and the advantages obtainable from unquoted businesses for particular third party interests and for the economy in general, unquoted businesses should be relieved of inheritance tax, either through the abolition of the tax or through a regime of exemption.

So it is clear that IHT will remain a political football for some time to come. A change of government may well adopt more punitive measures, as the Labour party is ideologically more inclined to the capital transfer tax concept, where the onus falls on the donor rather than the dependent or recipient.

That said, it is still a punitive regime if the appropriate measures are not taken at the right time. For example, the IHT burden on a chargeable estate of £500,000 can amount to £156,000.

The climate does allow gifts to be made over to dependents with fewer tax liabilities than ever before. In theory at least, IHT can be totally avoided if all of a person's assets are gifted and the donor survives for another seven years. It is doubtful whether anybody would actually do this, though. But for owners of family businesses, the balance that has to be struck is between retention of wealth and the transfer of that wealth.

Certain questions need to be asked and certain steps need to be taken. Do you want to give away the bulk of your assets during your lifetime or after your death? What do you intend to give to whom – and do those arrangements make provision for any change in your personal circumstances? (Such changes might include divorce or rifts with your children.)

Once those questions have been answered, a valuation has to be made of your assets, your capital position and your income. For many family businesses, the predominant part of that estate will be the value of the shares in the company.

If planning is not carried out, IHT can make a dramatic impression on the fortune of a company. Table 5.1 is taken from *Inheritance Tax: A practical guide*, published by Stoy Hayward (Stillerman, 1989).

As Barry Stillerman points out, this is easily not the worst case scenario. If business property relief was not applicable, the shortfall would have been £300,000. If 30 per cent business property relief had been available, the shortfall would have been £140,000. The impact of this would have been mitigated if the deceased in the example had gifted some shares in the family company eight years before his or her death (see Table 5.2).

As Stillerman points out, there are differing types of trust into which these shares can be placed. It may be that the owner does

Table 5.1 An estate of £1.6 million comprises a house worth £200,000, investments of £100,000 and shares in the family trading company worth £1.3 million

	£000
Value of estate	1,600
Business property relief, say, £1.3m × 50%	(650)
Chargeable estate	950
IHT	336
Sale of assets to pay the tax:	
House	200
Investments	100
	300
Shortfall	36

not want to lose control over the voting rights of the shares while wanting to pass on the wealth implicit in those shares.

Charitable trusts

Many family businesses favour the establishment of a charitable trust. This trust can be formed by the family and then controlled by a trustee from outside. It removes the wealth of the shares from the family (because the shares must be held for charitable

Table 5.2 Estate on death

	£000
House	200
Investments	100
Shares in family trading company	800
	1,100
Less business property relief at, say, 50%	(400)
	700
IHT (covered by value of house and investments)	236

purposes) but voting control remains with the family. Again, using the first example, see Table 5.3.

There are a number of forms of trust into which shares can be gifted. Most people who own shares in a family business – and particularly if they carry voting rights – will not wish to gift them straight over to their children. By doing that, any further influence on the direction of the company has been lost.

The options that most will consider are the bare trust, the accumulation trust, the interest in possession trust and the discretionary trust. While it will be up to financial advisers and individual circumstances to decide which is the most appropriate, the broad definitions are as follows:

1. The bare trust is, in essence, an outright gift to someone who has not reached majority age. Once reaching the age of 18, the beneficiary can demand that the assets be transferred.
2. The accumulation and maintenance trust enables parents to have control over their gift even though the beneficiary may be over the age of 18. There are a number of freedoms from an IHT charge provided that the beneficiary receives at least an interest in the income of the trust once over 25 and that

Table 5.3 Shares in the family trading company worth £180,000 are bequeathed to the family charitable trust on death: chargeable estate

	£000
Shares in family trading company	1,300
Less bequest of shares to charitable trust	(180)
Value of remaining shares, say	1,120
Less business property relief at, say, 50%	(560)
	560
House	200
Investments	100
	860
IHT thereon	300
Tax paid by sale of house and investments	300

the income of the trust is accumulated or applied for the maintenance, education or benefit of the beneficiary.

3. The interest in possession trust entails that the beneficiary has a right to the income of the trust from the outset. According to Barry Stillerman, they are useful 'if a person wishes to plan the method in which his wealth is to be distributed while ensuring that the capital is not squandered'.

4. The discretionary trust allows the benefactor to keep his or her options very open. The trustees have full discretion as to who receives income or capital and when such payments are made. For IHT purposes, though, it is regarded as being less flexible.

Employee share schemes

The 1980s saw a significant move towards wider share ownership, both through the privatisation programmes and through the promotion of share option schemes. The effects of these trends on family businesses can be pronounced.

Executives in public companies have now far greater incentives than mere salary. A family business that cannot match these incentives is likely to find itself outpaced and outmanoeuvred in the search for the best managers. There is a reverse side to this process: that the family business offers greater stability of employment at a time of merger and acquisition. However, the offer of a quieter life is not necessarily the signal that one needs to give to some managers who wish to be entrepreneurs within some form of corporate environment.

Savings-related share option schemes, profit sharing schemes and executive share option schemes are all widely available in public companies. The first two schemes are open to any employee. In the former, employees save for a five-year period with a building society or with the National Savings. At the end of the five years, they can cash their savings or use the proceeds to buy shares in the company based on their value at the start of the savings period. There is a limit as to how many shares can be purchased by an employee each month and there is a prescribed discount on the shares of 20 per cent. With a profit sharing scheme, the company buys its own shares for distribution to the employees, who receive them free of income tax, while the cost to the company is tax deductible.

Both these schemes are open to any employee who has served the company for five years (and there is scope for others to participate, on a discretionary basis).

The executive share option scheme, which has proved very popular, allows the company to determine who takes part and does not place any limit on the extent of their participation. Most public companies have an executive share option scheme.

But are they right for the family business? The crucial question that any such scheme begs is whether the family wants to lose part of its holding in the company. Not offering shares can be a disincentive. Offering shares can be both an administrative headache and an unnecessary irritant at times when the destiny of the company is being decided.

Naturally, the questions raised are related to the family's understanding of its long-term destiny. They are also related to the problem of how each member of the family is rewarded. In a family business, a shareholding is usually only passed from one member to another and that will be on the basis of an independent valuation of the shares. There are conflicts between buyer and seller as to which price most accurately resembles the market rate – one will think that they do not reflect the real value while the other, mindful of inheritance tax and the passing on of shares from one generation to the next, will wish to keep the price low. If these are delicate problems that face just two members of the family in a private transaction, then what complications could arise in an unquoted company with a number of employees also wanting to buy and sell their shareholding?

Exit routes

The ESOP

An important way forward is the formation of the Employee Share Ownership Plan, or ESOP. An ESOP represents an exit route for a family business should it want to divest itself, whether in part or in whole, of its ownership. Underlying the idea is the realisation that a family business may not want to go public but may want to make an exploratory move away from total control. At the same time, ceding any amount of control to an unauthorised or unknown person on the share register is anathema to most family businesses. So, the argument runs, why not offer a part of the company to those people who are already a part of the business and who are committed to it? The ESOP is not a commitment to sell out as much as a commitment to extend the family; the qualification, though, is not that of marriage but of being part of the business.

However, if employees are to be let in to the ownership of the firm, whether it be one, six or a lot, they will not wish to end up in the position that many families can find themselves – paper rich and cash hungry. Employees have to have a way out; eventually they will die or retire and will want to sell their shares. Unlike the family, they may not want to hand them to their children. The role of the ESOP is to act as a kind of market maker. ESOPs may be attractive for the public company because they employ existing shares instead of new ones as a way of raising money and because they represent a safe home for those shares. However, for many of those who have devised and promoted the concept, ESOPs were fundamentally for the family firm in the UK.

The ESOP has quite a long history in the United States but it is rather a different animal there. Its growth in the past five years has been largely tax-driven – if a bank lends to an ESOP, for example, half of its interest earnings do not count as taxable income for the bank. Indeed, it has reached the point where ESOPs have acquired something of a bad name in the United States. They were seen as merely an easy form of defence for a large company faced with a takeover bid. They have been thought to entrench management while offering little extra motivation for enhanced productivity. Some more appropriate schemes for management have been ignored in the stampede towards ESOPs.

In the United Kingdom, although the name is the same the situation is different – as is the tax environment. Here we are building on ten years of individual employee share ownership plans. The ESOP is basically a discretionary trust established for the employees of a company. The trust is funded by contributions from the company itself, external borrowing or even by a loan from the company. The ESOP then acquires shares in the business, either by subscribing for shares or by making a market and acquiring shares from those employees who wish to sell. The shares acquired by the trust are then available for distribution back to employees within the company.

The cultural hurdles that the ESOP faces are quite high, and they have not just been among the left wing of political thought. Directors and owners of companies have expressed their doubts over the influence of a large collective bloc of employee-shareholder votes ranged against them. ESOPs could lead to a weakening of management, it is believed.

The reluctance of the family business to offer individual share schemes or profit share schemes has been a driving force for the implementation of ESOPs in the United Kingdom.

While proponents of the ESOP made it clear to the government that they didn't mind the legislation being limited to non-PLCs, it appears that the government has been slightly embarrassed that after ten years of share ownership all the share schemes are run by public companies. Because of the unmarketability of their shares, the private family business could not and would not let go. Since the rates for income tax and capital gains tax are now the same, the family business has preferred to use cash rather than shares as an incentive. Furthermore, those executives were not taking shares because there was not a market for them.

So the argument for ESOPs was carried on the basis that family businesses had not implemented share schemes.

What has been the demand for them since they were made available? The answer so far is: a lot of unfocused interest. Perhaps many firms knew what they wanted.

One ESOP consultant recalls getting sixty chief executives to a seminar. Their reaction? It answered their needs but it sounded too good to be true.

In effect, the ESOP trust could borrow from a bank, buy the shares off the family and then get capital gains tax treatment. The company has acquired the family's shares through debt; when the company pays off the debt through the trust, both the interest and the capital are tax-deductible.

In the mid-1980s two forms of interest were shown. There were those who felt that they had to compete. At that time, the bull market was very strong and everybody was advertising their share option schemes. Private companies couldn't just sit back and say that it didn't matter. The other group were those who wanted to get out. They were family members who wanted to sell and for whom the only obstacle was their loyalty to grandad.

Since then the take-up among the private company sector has not been as extensive as the ESOP supporters would have liked. They believe that further tax breaks may be needed, preferably in the form of some holdover relief. For example, it is argued that, when a family sells to a quoted company, it gets paper and lower capital gains tax. Can this principle be extended? In the US, if a family sells to an ESOP and gets money which they then invest in the US market they get a rollover. This, too, is a point of debate. Perhaps there just is not quite enough in it for the family at the moment.

There is a further difficulty for the promoters of the ESOP – valuation. The family will want to sell a stake at the best possible price. Yet they will not want to upset the valuation placed on the shares that are to be handed on to the next generation. On the one hand, they want a low price; on the other, they want a high price. There is no clear resolution to this one. The family will have to face this issue head on if it wants to dispose of its shares anyway. The tax problems of maintaining a low valuation won't go away.

Case study: Lucas Furniture and the ESOP   One example of a family business ESOP is that of Lucas Furniture Industries, a third generation business based in the East End of London. At the end of 1989 the company had a turnover of £11 million and projected that to increase to £23 million by 1992; profits stood at £420,000 and were envisaged to rise to £700–800,000. It employs nearly 200 people.

Like many other East End furniture companies, Lucas was founded at the turn of the century by a Russian emigré. Lucas is the only London-based company of its kind now left and the family takes a special pride in its survival. Says its chief executive Jack Lucas:

We have watched our contemporaries lose their independence in this sector. We are really the last of the Mohicans. Parallel companies have been merged or submerged and their fate has strengthened our resolve to maintain our future under our own control. It's a bit of a David versus Goliath syndrome, and I think that employee participation represents the ultimate commitment to that desire for independence. The ESOP is just one, but highly important, element in our strategy.

In Lucas' instance, one million new shares have been created, which equates to an equity stake of nearly 11.5 per cent. The shares have been set aside in an ESOP, to encourage as many employees as possible to become shareholders. The shares are held by a trust company, Lucas Trustees, and are made available for subscription to qualifying employees over a planned period.

(Twelve months' service is the qualification and there is no ceiling on individual share ownership.)

The scheme was launched with an initial distribution by the trustees. Just over 27,000 shares were set aside and each participating employee was given 150 shares without cost. Previously there were 22 shareholders and most are still involved; family and non-family management control over 50 per cent of the company.

'We want to encourage a handing back of the shares into the pot', says Jack Lucas, 'but whether we can insist on that is a thorny issue.'

Conceptually, then, for Lucas, the ESOP represents a reservoir of shares that can have a value for the employees – because they can identify with the prospects of the company by participating in the scheme – while at the same time not having a value for an outside company. The shares can be parked in the ESOP until suitable employees take them up. At the same time, it has enabled the Lucas family to restructure the company.

These are early days for the UK ESOP. They do offer a neat way with which shares in a company can be recycled, particularly when the share structure has become dispersed and diluted after a few generations.

But are family firms culturally inclined to give shares to their employees? Some observers think that not many of them are. Plenty of family businesses may have to be dragged screaming into this arena. Supporters of ESOPs will argue that it is an inevitable process; it might take twenty years but the trend is towards individual, direct ownership. It may be that the thrust to greater individualism is too far down the road for family businesses to stop it. Private companies are not immune to general cultural pressure. The ESOP bandwagon seems likely to roll only at the pace at which family firms find that they need it to roll.

This is recognised by one expert:

You can use company profits to fund it. But traditionally, private companies have been able to depress their profits very successfully, often by pushing their money into pension funds. But if pension funds are overfunded and corporation tax is low, there may be more of an inclination to have more declarable profits. There is, however, a large inertia factor.

One major problem is that the trustees of an ESOP must comprise a majority of workers who are not and never have been directors. For a lot of traditional family businesses that would be anathema.

Management buy-outs

In some cases, the management buy-out is the ideal exit route for the family business. In the use of the management buy-out (or MBO) the United Kingdom is ahead of the rest of Europe. Their growth has been explosive. The number of MBOs of listed and un-listed companies valued at over £10 million jumped from twenty-two in 1985 to forty-seven in the first nine months of 1989; the value of these deals rose from £850 million to £4,950 million.

Although the MBO has proved to be vulnerable to long periods of high interest rates, there can be little doubt of the willingness of managements to try. The reasons are straightforward enough: the MBO gives management the chance to own their business. While the market may still be attracted by the occasional spectacular deal, it is the steady flow of smaller transactions that is subtly changing the pattern of British business ownership. According to Peat Marwick McLintock, an estimated 300 deals valued at £5.41 billion were finalised between January and mid-September in 1989. In other words, a lot of small deals are occurring.

The Centre for Management Buy-Out Research at the University of Nottingham notes that there is a growing trend for family businesses to engage in MBOs. In 1988, MBOs of family businesses accounted for 27.8 per cent of the market, the highest percentage share ever recorded.

The MBO offers a new angle on the old problem. It can be hard to sustain the inheritance of the family business, particularly if the next generation is not interested in joining the business. The outgoing generation would then have looked for a purchaser of the business. With the MBO, they can look to the management as a potential purchaser.

A diluted shareholding throughout many generations means that the managers have no ownership. Yet, if the shares are to be redistributed among the managers, the family members' wishes have to be met. Some family members will want income and others will want capital. It has to be done carefully. But one of the biggest hurdles that the venture capital and funding institutions can find is that there is no impetus to get it done; there may be no momentum behind the commercial decisions.

For a major institution such as 3i, MBOs in family businesses represent a small but reasonable chunk of its annual work – perhaps 14 per cent or so. It makes approximately 1,000 investments yearly, distilled from about 10,000 enquiries. Of those, perhaps 5,000 are fairly serious. Half of those will reach the stage of triggering internal procedures; then either 3i will reject the company or the company will reject 3i. And 3i is seeing renewed interest among private companies in developing and growing with strategic intent and not just 'chugging along'. The company runs a three-day course on 'Your private business' and every year it is oversubscribed. 'Perhaps the MBO is one of the best things to have happened to family businesses', says 3i's Gail Croston.

'I don't think that the MBO changes the culture of the family business', says David Franks of accountants Blackstone Franks. 'If anything, it supports it. It boosts loyalty and it gives resource to that expression of loyalty.' He continues:

The 1988 Finance Act made a huge difference to people's perceptions. Up to that point the perceived knowledge was that you earned money, got a lot of dividend and paid a lot of tax. You then sold the business. You had to think of retirement and security. Now that position has been eroded. The view is now that you might as well hang on to the business. The only reason for going public is to acquire other companies rather than to cash in, as was the case. And lots of family firms don't want to acquire other businesses. You have a nice little business which is doing well and which, if you wished, you could sell later.

The point, says Franks, is that if the family does not wish to retain the company within the family structure, it can now be sold to the management. For one thing, the family knows and likes the managers and will be comfortable with the sale. Secondly, there are none of the indemnities and warranties that a purchasing company can insist on.

Case study: a successful MBO It was an old and established manufacturing business. Now over 150 years old, it had expanded beyond the United Kingdom into a number of far-flung overseas markets. The family still controlled 100 per cent of the equity.

The family had received a number of offers for the company. Some of them had been tempting, particularly because neither of the two brothers had an heir apparent for the business. The family had always prided itself on quality of product and had also pursued a policy of growth that they considered marked them out from so many unadventurous family firms in their sector. However, turnover was slowing down and profits were sluggish. The overseas ventures were proving to be more of a drain than an opportunity. High profile orders were taken but for little or no margin. It kept the company's name in the headlines but it did little for the balance sheet.

The situation was exasperating for the chief executive, who had been brought in from outside a few years before. He was proud to be associated with the family and its company, having always had a respect for its products, but he was not so proud of the family's refusal to see that a change of culture was needed if the firm was to remain competitive. From the chief executive's point of view, the brothers were playing at the business and this percolated down through the management – there simply was not enough profit motive.

The way forward was an MBO. The chief executive talked to several of his senior managers. Were they willing to invest tens of thousands of their own money in the scheme? But that would scarcely account for the sums needed to buy control from the family. So the chief executive talked to a number of venture capital institutions; for £2.5 million they would have the first option on the company should the management team fail. The institutions said that they were interested.

The chief executive proposed the plan at the next board meeting. He and his managers would take over one-third of the company as would the institutions. The remainder would be left with the family. As far as the brothers were concerned, it was an ideal solution. They had withdrawn from the day-to-day running of the business two years before; now they had an opportunity to remain independent, retain the family name above the door and yet – with a freshly motivated management team – make a much better return from their reduced shareholding. Their cake would be smaller but would contain rather more richness.

Once the brothers elected to support the buy-out, events moved quickly. The buy-out deal had to be constructed and put to the board while a business plan had to go to the institutions. Within weeks, the brothers and the management team had signed an outline agreement and the buy-out was completed a month later.

Several months later the original team of management shareholders was joined by many others. The company is looking
to extend that ownership still further. The company's finances
are much improved; the foreign ventures have been sold or cut
back to realistic levels. Profits have become the driving force of
the company – and the brothers are happy with their ongoing
investment.

The MBO is likely to have a particularly bright future on main-
land Europe, where there are many thousands of family owned
businesses established after the Second World War. About one
in four of the 40,000 French companies employing between 50
and 1,000 people will be changing ownership because of the
proprietor reaching retirement age. For many family firms, the
attraction will be that the deal can be achieved quickly and with
confidence. After all, many proprietors do not want to hawk their
life's achievement about the market-place like some cheap item
of merchandise.

Often the MBO will lead to a flotation or to a sale. What the
MBO does is place a majority of the ownership either in the hands
of directors or in the hands of investing institutions. It is likely,
therefore, that the MBO will prove to be a staging post in the
company's history. Some will argue that employee share ownership will gradually take over from director/institution ownership;
others believe that the rate of return on investment will naturally
continue to decline from its heady peak of 40 per cent in 1987.

There are many family businesses which have recognised that
their particular market is changing fundamentally. Many small
firms are being replaced by one large firm. Economies of scale are
required. For the family business that wishes to retain a presence
in the market-place, the MBO may only be the first step.

Case study: from family to management ownership   'We
may remain a private company but it will, to a fair old extent,
lose its family nature', one managing director told me, although
he himself was retaining a 20 per cent stake in the firm.

His company is a very good example of the transitions that are
occurring in many family businesses. For the sake of clarity, I
shall refer to him as Brian.

It is a long-established affair, founded in the early years of the
nineteenth century. In the middle of last century the firm joined

forces with another family business; it was a partnership that was to last well over 100 years. When Brian joined his father in the late 1960s, he was under orders to develop a new leg for the business. Since then, a third leg has been added. Now all three are roughly similar in size. They are run autonomously; Brian, an outside director and one or two group executives provide a centralised service. 'They are run as independently as possible, just using group funding and some marketing ideas', Brian explains. 'Each of the managing directors has been made a director of the group.' Yet the firm is facing a period of considerable change. Why?

At the end of the 1970s the shares had been split over a wide range of family trusts, reflecting the heritage of two sets of families for over 100 years. Brian and his brother, along with their father (who was then chairman), held only 20 per cent. On the other family's side, there was tragedy when the last of the line was killed in a car crash. They wanted to realise their shareholding as they no longer had an active involvement in the company.

These circumstances allowed Brian to persuade his brother and his father that they should buy out all the existing shareholders. This they did with the assistance of an investing institution, which held nearly 25 per cent of the company.

It was the right thing to have done. The only problem was that there was a major recession looming. 'The only graph I had known was an upwards one', says Brian, 'and the world fell through in the early eighties. There were high interest charges and markets that we were heavily into just folded. We had a very torrid time for about three years.'

Attempts were made at diversification, but one went wrong. That mistake forced Brian to face his brother and father. 'I said that we weren't running the company in the way that we had to. We had got to develop a large organisation; we needed more professional management and we had to make it more attractive for them to come in and join us.'

A non-executive director and an outside executive director were introduced. A more formalised business structure was developed. As this new way of running the company evolved, so it became clear that Brian's brother was uncomfortable with these changes. He bought out a part of the business.

Brian went away to business school. It coincided with his father retiring. A non-executive chairman was put in. As Brian explains:

With hindsight it was probably not the best thing to have done. My father no longer relished the job in the way he had and so was quite prepared to relinquish things. So we needed someone to look after the family's interests while I was away. I would then return and take over. But the family found that their best interests were not being served. I believe that the chairman had more of an eye on the interests of the investing institution than on those of the family. He was, after all, a City man and had come to us with the institution's recommendation. We were not controlling matters as effectively as we wished to do.

Brian was faced with a dilemma. He could watch the chairman take the company in a direction that he believed was not serving the family's interests, or he could try to buy out the institution and find other backers. He chose the latter option.

'I expressed a preference to stay here and take out a smaller chunk of the business. That way we realised a part of our investment for my father but I could still see the business working.' Other venture capitalists were brought in and so, crucially, were some of the other managers. His brother and his father have supported the action. Now Brian is intending to go for a flotation.

We need the cash. The requirement for that funding was going to dilute our family interest further in any case; the need for investment was obvious. But also, the market had changed. The industries that we are in have moved from being run by lots of small fish to a few large fish. The combination of our disappointment with the chairman, combined with the need for investment, have led me to this conclusion. Once we have gone for the quote, I hope that my father and my brother will climb back in with a stake and hopefully that will give better value than their old shareholding. It means that my father can enjoy his retirement but does not have the sadness of seeing his company go completely. He would have an interest in the company and will continue to support me.

Flotation

For some family businesses, flotation has been the liberating influence that they were looking for. It may seem surprising to others that families are willing to undergo this particularly gruelling rite of passage.

Flotation takes up weeks and weeks of senior management time. It costs a lot and many believe that it can cripple long-term planning. As one financial director once said: 'It's a funny process You have to present the company's history to a degree of accuracy that can drive you nutty. For the first time in your life you feel that you are not in control of your advisers; they grill you – and you pay them a fee for the privilege.'

There are classic reasons for going public. Realisation of existing investment and the ability to raise capital through the issuing of paper are perhaps the most powerful arguments. On top of that, many companies find that their status is enhanced among their customers and that employee share schemes become that much more attractive.

Flotation is not the only route, as I have tried to make clear. Companies can opt for private placings of their shares (possibly via the Business Expansion Scheme), although this does not create marketable paper. Should the prime motivation be investment realisation, the share sale to an ESOP might be considered. More drastically, the family can sell its business outright.

The realisation issue is particularly critical for family firms. By the fifth generation you could have well over eighty members of a family. How do you divide the rewards between employers and shareholders? The advantage of a listing is that it brings the problem to a full stop. There may be battles within a company, with some directors wanting to keep things the way they are, but placing some shares in the market can give a complete generation in which to change the company's character. With a 40 per cent cohesive stake, the family can effectively hold control. It's not as absolute as a sale.

The profile of the type of company coming to market is changing. The growth in MBOs has created numerous businesses that, from the moment of inception, are preparing for flotation in order to realise the investment made by their financial backers. Their genetic structure has been coded from birth. But such companies are still in the relative minority. Many stockbrokers will still be dealing principally with family firms.

One thing that the family firm quickly learns is that they will have underestimated the amount of work and the change in attitude required in the run-up to flotation. Says one broker:

The earlier we get to know a company, the better. For them, it can be quite a learning curve. Some find the questions that have to be answered if not embarrassing, then certainly tough. In some cases, existing financial controls might be archaic, seat of the pants stuff.

Many private companies have lived for many years having only to fulfil minimum statutory requirements; the shock of half-year results, preliminary announcements and additional disclosures can be quite great.

'Directors vastly underestimate the efforts and the effects of change', says David Carter, head of corporate finance services at KPMG Peat Marwick McLintock. 'We would encourage thinking that looks three years ahead. What's needed is fairly obvious, so do it well in advance. Suppose you have been conservative in your stock counting. That has got to be changed, but not in the final year, when it would affect profits. Inheritance tax planning has also to be well managed ahead.'

Flotation is expensive. It can cost anywhere between £125,000 and £300,000, depending on the size of the flotation. It is easy to spend a lot more than you normally would.

Procedures gobble up time. One financial director recalls that he thought it would take one person one full week to write the prospectus. As week followed week of 7 a.m. to 10 p.m. days, the world seemed to become ever more unreasonable. For months there was little else to think about. It is also tortuous in the complexity of meetings; meetings will involve the sponsoring merchant bank, the stockbroker, two sets of solicitors and one or two sets of accountants. On top of that there are ancillary services – PR advisers, pension advisers, property valuers. Typically there may be ten meetings and about ten or fifteen proofs of the document. Then the directors have to warrant, line by line, that everything is true. Every sentence carries a point that needs verifying to some degree.

After the flotation, the management has to live with a new set of circumstances. What was a private world has partly pulled the curtains back and is admitting some light. Most companies will use the analogy of the goldfish bowl. PR awareness has to be nurtured. Actions have to be explained. The observer's point of view has to be taken into account. Statements have to be made and mulled over. While it may be easier to acquire other businesses, it might be more difficult to inform (and, perhaps, obtain approval from) shareholders about non-trading activities and deals. The firm has to be conscious of its investors because the decisions that are made are not just for the family, or its previous proprietors. 'It certainly makes you think a little more', says one finance director of a quoted family business.

There are other minor potential disadvantages. The implications for one's personal taxation are neutral but there are possible liabilities for any vendor shareholders. It is inadvisable, for example, to die just after floating your company. The greater demands on record keeping might become a bureaucratic disadvantage. The checks and balances imposed by the investing work can be constraining for some entrepreneurial spirits – but that is more a question of temperament than anything else.

Entrepreneurial role models   It may be significant that two entrepreneurial role models whose achievements have lasted longer than those of other heroes of business in the 1980s were men who have built upon their family business and who have used the capital markets to do so.

Gerald Ratner and Howard Hodgson have both established dominance in their fields after inheriting small, comfortable businesses that needed fresh impetus and direction if they were to survive. Flotation, acquisition and a toughly competitive view of the world have achieved those aims.

Gerald Ratner took over the family business from his father in 1984, having joined the firm straight from school. There was no other choice as far as he was concerned – the jewellery trade was in the blood. His parents ran the shop and talked about the business with him before putting him in charge of a warehouse, where results improved dramatically.

While his father ran the business at a profit, selling jewellery on a value-for-money basis, his son intended greater things. The old, forbidding nature of the jewellery stores – with their 'once in a lifetime' feeling – was dismembered. Young people were encouraged to come in and spend their money regularly. The ethos of the street trader rather than the snooty manner of the waistcoated expert was introduced. Price became all-important.

Soon thereafter Ratner started to buy up the competition – Terry's, H. Samuel, Ernest Jones, Zales and Salisbury's in the United Kingdom, together with Sterling and Westhall in the United States. One in three watches and one in four engagement rings bought in the United Kingdom now come from a store owned by Ratner Group and it is intended that the company should capture 50 per cent of the UK market.

In 1980 Hodgson Holdings was a small family firm performing 1,000 funerals each year. Howard Hodgson, the fifth generation of

Hodgson to enter the business, was directing many of the funerals himself. In 1986 he took the company public and became the second largest funeral directing business in the United Kingdom after the Co-op. In 1989 Hodgson Holdings was involved in a three-way tie-up between Kenyon Securities (one of the other quoted funeral directors) and Pompes Funèbres Générales of France, creating PHK International, one of the major funeral directing companies in Europe. At the time of the merger, pre-tax profits stood at £3.4 million.

Hodgson went into the family business in the late 1960s but there were ructions between him and his father. 'At that time I was really rather poor', he recalls, 'and I was getting used to a life of mild and dominoes.' It also left him with 'a raging fire to buy my father up'. Which he did in 1975.

On the first morning he was told that the company was insolvent and that the bank manager was closing it down. Hodgson obtained a £5,000 extension to the overdraft. 'The roof was leaking and the cars wouldn't start. The hearses were held together by welded coffin plates. It was pure bloody disaster. I ran off to buy turnover.' The first acquisition added more funerals and Hodgson was off. At the same time, Hodgson acknowledges the influence of his father. 'He was a professionally qualified mortician. The knowledge and professionalism that we have put into this company owes as much to my father as it does to me. I had that culture of good standards drummed into me as a child.'

Outrageous self-belief and a passionate belief in service have inspired Hodgson's climb to the top. Funeral companies have traditionally been family run businesses. What Hodgson brought – along with the Field family of Great Southern Group – was a recognition that here was an industry that needed economies of scale. While the four largest groups control between 40 and 50 per cent of the UK funeral market, the remainder is in the hands of nearly 2,500 independent operations. Under current conditions, it is unlikely to be profitable to direct fewer than 200 funerals each year.

The family nature of the business has played a crucial part in the shape of the industry. In the past, it was simply presumed that the new generation would follow the old. Each business developed a considerable loyalty within the locality that it served, regardless, as Hodgson points out, of 'whether the service was good, bad or indifferent'. But funeral directing is scarcely the most attractive business for children to join. Many family funeral businesses are faced with a succession problem on account of the image of the job, and many have simply given up trading in the past few years once the head of the family has retired.

Hodgson identified certain areas through which the business could be built. Market share had to be increased; the only feasible way of doing that was through acquisition. This is because of the extensive goodwill that is developed by each funeral director: most people use a particular firm on the basis of previous knowledge. It is not an area in which customers 'shop around'.

Through the building up of market share, economies of scale began to flow through. Facilities could be rationalised, fixed costs could be controlled, and a wider range of facilities and services could be introduced. Administration and finance could be centralised and fleets of hearses could be pooled. Items such as floral and monumental masonry work could be offered at more competitive rates.

In addition, stronger management control could be instilled. At Hodgson Holdings rigorous reporting meetings are held most days. Says Hodgson:

This business was structured out of going bankrupt. It had some good structures and systems in terms of funeral operations. We needed to expand and get economies of scale. And among most of the businesses we have bought there has been something that was better than our own method – so we have adopted it. The day we think that we can't change anything because it's all so good is the day we have to resign.

Hodgson is proud of one Coopers & Lybrand report conducted two years ago on behalf of a prospective bidder. 'It was a long form report that said that this was one of the best hands-on management systems in the UK. The information goes down, comes back, and we have an ability to turn the company's direction. It's a middle management structure that actually makes things happen.'

Hodgson challenges many assumptions that many people – both inside and outside funeral directing – had about the nature of the profession. He has spent his last decade buying family businesses. It was considered a quiet, honourable service. Like Gerald Ratner, he has outraged many traditional elements.

I reject the idea that you can only be a little, middle-aged man owning your own business to be any good. But small family run funeral directors have traded on this. 'At least I own my business and therefore I care' is their line. That is rubbish. It's amazing how often after buying a firm that the owner – who is now the manager – phones you on the first Monday morning and says 'we need new livery, new vehicles, a vacuum cleaner, a kettle for the staff.' Apparently they didn't need any of those things last week when he owned the business but now they are crucial. There was a conflict – it was called his pocket.

To reflect these changing times, a British Institute of Funeral Directors has been set up. It's for qualified non-owners. 'They talk more sensibly than the National Association of Funeral Directors where you have to be the owner', Hodgson says.

He is also keenly aware of the image of the business, how this affects relationships between parents and children, and how it will affect long-term recruiting policy. It is a perception based on personal experience.

The old image has to go. When you go to school you are asked what your father does. No, he isn't a bank manager or an accountant or a businessman, he's a funeral director. And they would all say 'how horrid for you'. Then you wouldn't get kissed under the mistletoe because you might have been touching dead bodies that week. So there was that rather distasteful enigma. Yes, we have bleepers and answerphones but you can't get away from the fact that it's a 24-hour day every day of the year and this is the age of leisure. And it will always be the son who wears the bleeper. So he doesn't have any fun. Yet he could put up with all of this *if his father was actually making any damn money.*

Sale

The ultimate answer for any family wanting to get out of the business which they have built or inherited is to sell it. As we have seen above, there are plenty of funeral directors who have made just such a decision.

It is not an easy decision, nor is it as simple as it sounds. For one thing, there are strong emotions at work. Secondly, it is difficult to identify the right purchaser. It takes a lot of time and effort. And then there is the question of inexperience – vendors usually have not sold a business before and they will probably only do it once.

There are all manner of vendors. There are those who want to sell because they do not want to become, as they see it, merely an administrator. There are those who want to stay and grow with the business but who need to be part of a larger empire to achieve those goals. The family wealth may be tied up in the business but the earn-out that can be received means that some secure cash in the bank can be guaranteed for the family.

For many family firms the USM route may not be the right one – there are quite a few companies that are too small for the USM. The danger is that there is too much pressure and firms end up not using their paper, which is why they floated in the first place.

So why sell? For a family business, there is usually one strong reason: that the next generation of the family is either incapable or unwilling to take over the reins, or because the incumbent owner has no children. Sale can also occur if there is a desire for expansion that cannot be met out of existing shareholders' funds and where the borrowing requirement is too high. For some companies, it may prove to be a more appropriate answer than a flotation.

From the point of view of the vendor, there are a number of criteria that must be considered in order to present a favourable picture to possible purchasers and which will help to obtain the best possible price and conditions for sale.

There is no such thing as the perfect company, even though years of involvement with it can lead the vendor to believe this to be the case. The methods by which the family has run the firm, though successful, may not be the methods by which a purchaser wishes to run it. While the purchaser is going to have to show a degree of flexibility in order to retain the management staff, it is also incumbent upon the family business to recognise the need for change.

The family should have a good idea of how much they might expect to receive for the company. In many areas of business there may not be a public company equivalent against which to compare your price/earnings multiple, but approximate examples should be researched. Here, the employment of specialist advisers would be recommended.

As far as the purchaser is concerned, a comprehensive investigation of your corporate state of health is going to be a prerequisite. The purchaser is going to want to know your short- and medium-term prospects as well as the current state of your bank balance.

The purchaser is going to be looking for the negatives with which to beat down the price. He will look for vulnerable areas and whether the overall state of the market which you are in is heading up or down. He will want to know how the stocks are valued and whether they can be considered as an undervalued asset. He will want to know about the management styles, financial controls, the use of information technology and customer contracts. A particularly sensitive area will be the executive perks – the purchaser may regard the company aeroplane as an unnecessary item. Similarly, the purchaser will want to know about the relationships that you have with any unions.

There will no doubt be times when the questions seem either impertinent or unnecessarily intrusive. They will want to look at the internal management accounts away from the site of the business. Everything from incentive schemes, distribution rights and pollution liability will come under the microscope. Profit forecasts and sales projections will be required.

Then comes the issue of valuation. There is, naturally, not going to be one answer. One side will think the price too high, the other will consider it too low. As far as a prospective vendor is concerned, it is important to understand upon what criteria the purchaser will be basing his decisions. The basis for his valuation will be that of the current balance sheet and assets, plus the future profits and cash flows. The criteria will be the earnings multiple, the discounted cash flow analysis, the return on capital employed, the earnings per share and the assets. There may well be factors other than these strictly financial ones; if the company is the only one of its kind or is the undisputed market leader in its sector, then the vendor has far greater leverage.

Before the final negotiations, the vendor should be clear about his aims and wishes regarding the following:

1. How the valuation has been arrived at.
2. The nature of any earn-out deal and how much of the purchase consideration is to be paid initially.
3. Who is to remain as a director of the firm and in what executive capacity.
4. Redundancy arrangements.
5. The fate of any valuable assets such as, say, a company flat.
6. The tax implications of the sale.

And then the sale is negotiated. The purchaser will want to know of any major pieces of news relating to the company that have occurred since the previous meeting. Retirement and salary packages and other service contracts will have to be discussed;

assets, premises and key customers will probably also feature; warranties and indemnities will be established. Only then is the purchase price agreed; the purchaser will have a maximum price in his mind, the vendor a minimum. Once that has been agreed, a timetable for legal completion is set.

For the vendor, there are some key guidelines. The purchase must coincide with his own tax needs, and in particular the impact of capital gains tax on large shareholders must be known. He must have a set of priorities; certain aspects of the sale are going to be more important than others to him – he has to know which they are. And he must always have at least one specialist adviser to hand at all times.

Case study: a decision to sell   The chairman represents the sixth generation to be involved in this manufacturing business. He has one son, who is only 12. He has a brother with one son and there is no sign that he wants to get his hands dirty – he is, in the chairman's words, 'an overqualified and underpaid academic'. His cousin also has one son, and he too is not seriously interested. Says the chairman:

I have largely decided, and have reasonably assumed, that there is not going to be a seventh generation, and that opens other opportunities. I see no particular point in keeping it private. Continuity is impossible, so it should now logically be a part of another company. And everyone keeps asking me 'why?' They all think, 'how wonderful, a sixth generation firm' and they derive a warm emotional glow. You can't be tempted by that. It would be quite nice to merge with another family business.

A number of things impinge on the timescale that I have mapped out. First, we have got to survive the current problem of interest rates. Then we have a major anniversary coming up and there is a bit of PR mileage to be made out of that. I have always wanted to retire from active chairmanship at the age of 60 but I have felt increasingly that maybe I should retire a little earlier than that in order to pursue other interests. So I guess that it will be in the next five years but it may be sooner rather than later.

I would actually be quite an important part in any sale that took place because there is a practical benefit in having not only the knowledge and the experience but in having the name in the company.

The other shareholders are happy enough provided that the deal is reasonable. I have a price in mind; I have posed the question to the annual general meeting and they are all aware of my intentions. Apart from the emotion of wishing for continuity, there was a recognition that it made sense. It was bound to be emotional, but if you look at the figures there was only one argument. If you reversed the question and said to a shareholder: 'Would you invest in this company?' the answer would be 'no'. Therefore staying in its current form clearly made no sense. How long did it take to reach this decision? That's very hard to answer. In the case of the other shareholders they didn't have much time. But I had been coming to it over a long number of years. We increased our authorised share capital to make an acquisition. I saw that it would dilute our control. At that point, you start to realise that life might change. Also, our non-executive director, who was also from a family business background, had persuaded his father to sell his company on the basis that he couldn't see a future for it. The point that he made to me was: 'What is the benefit to me and the next generation to have thirty years of hassle and then pass it on? Is that a practical solution? Put like that, the answer had to be that it wasn't and that it all seemed rather silly.

The final twist was when I addressed where we were going and how we might go forward. In other words, succession. That was the telling point. Once I saw that succession was not just likely to be a serious problem but unlikely to take place in family terms, that eased the other decisions considerably. If I had a son who had said 'Yes, I want to come into the business' it would have been much harder. I might have made the same decision, come to that, but it would have been very much harder.

6 Using external resources

The main problem here is not so much that family businesses have trouble when consulting them, but that they do not consult at all. Although most firms have their accountant and their lawyer, family businesses do not get the most out of them. They do not call them in, or when they do, they do not listen to them! (Stoy Hayward, 1989, p. 34)

There may be some self-pleading in the above remark but it does seem to be the case that there is a lingering suspicion of consultancy professions within many family firms. That said, there is also a lingering suspicion among the consultancy profession about family businesses. 'Don't talk to me about them', one eminent management consultant said to me, 'as they are nothing but trouble. They either don't tell you anything and waste time and money or they embroil you in their family politics.'

The truth, as ever, lies somewhere in the middle. Many family businesses employ consultants effectively. Others do without them at all. The art that many businesses and consultants have to learn is how to start the relationship off on the right foot. (When discussing consultants, I am assuming that they are other than the accountant, lawyer and banker who provide statutory functions for the company.)

To some degree, the consultant can be a stepping stone towards the employment of a non-executive director. Their appointment has to be made purely on commercial grounds, rather than as an arbiter for issues that only the family can resolve. The fundamental point that has to be made is that anybody who is invited to act as a consultant must not be a personal friend of the family. In that way lie introversion and thorny problems should their advice be at fault. One chairman observed:

In our early days we had some very bad professional advice, and our advisers were friends. Now you should never do that. Never. You have

102

advisers where you don't feel any embarrassment about telling them that you have made an unholy mess of something. The bad advice that we received set us back years. It taught me that you have to get the best possible advice – we lost nearly £50,000 from not doing so. But it was accepted at the time because it was coming from a friend at the time – he isn't any longer!

At the time my father was losing a little of his impetus and yet I was still inexperienced. What this adviser told me struck me as being pretty stupid but I didn't have the experience to counter it. Now, if we had got good quality advice, telling us that we were in trouble, it would have encouraged my father and I to do something about it. As it was, we were lulled into a sense of false security. It seems silly now, but when I was 20 and this adviser was 30 years or so older, I thought that I could have been worrying unduly.

In this instance, the experience was a salutary one. The chairman has both a board that is entirely non-family and a team of professional advisers.

Culture versus the consultant

The culture of the family firm does to some extent militate against the use of consultants. The founder, strong-willed and entrepreneurial, has no time – and, in his eyes, no proven need – for an outside consultant. He has little need for an outsider because the outsider cannot bring any new insights to his business. There is also the distrust of those who consult among those who 'do'; the consultant is an unnecessary frippery. It is in the family firm that the axiom of consultants being those who borrow your watch to tell you the time can have the greatest credence.

It is hard and often impossible to penetrate such attitudes. The arguments are clear: no business will make it, and continue to make it, unless they employ good quality advice. Family firms need the discipline of professional lawyers, accountants or insurers. Such advisers are not there for comparison's sake or for taking risks or rewards.

The disciplines that consultants can impose are numerous. Some small family businesses may be in need of a vision as to where they should be aiming and, furthermore, in need of advice as to how to achieve that. Small family businesses are often those with thin financial information available to them; the audit is a necessary evil but constant monitoring and awareness of cash flow is just plain necessity. Family companies with a sense of purpose and drive can often lose sight of administrative details in favour of the work in progress. The training procedures within family companies can be limited and introduction to case studies – and reference to other family business problems – can help in the teaching and development of the new generation.

As the Stoy Hayward report summarises: the outside expert can help/plan issues of succession or changes to the management structure; can act as an evaluator of family members and their performance within the firm; and can assist in the management of growth and change. But more than one observer has commented that such desirable objectives are not always regarded by family firms as being achievable through the use of consultants. Indeed, some firms see such outside assistance as inimical to help. This attitude is thankfully not as common as it was, but there is no denying that it still exists.

Family-controlled firms are tough clients. Most consultants, even experienced ones, get caught in two critical contradictions unique to family-controlled firms. The first is the conflict between the pragmatic, here-and-now needs of the firm and the longer-range, emotional needs of the family members. The second conflict is between the different overlapping spheres of influence – family members, other owners, managers and employees – all of which are in conflict with one another for resources. (Robert Metzger, *Journal of Management Consulting*, 1988, vol. 4, no. 4, p. 15)

The other problem for consultants, identified by many students of family firms, is that of secrecy. To the family members, the consultant is an intruder who is in the position of obtaining financial information that is supremely confidential; therefore, even if the consultant is employed, little information will be divulged. The consultant is thus unable to make fully informed decisions and is soon dismissed as irrelevant and as having been a waste of time. Yet again, the first hurdle of trust has proved as insurmountable as Becher's Brook.

'Consultants don't tell you anything. They come in, learn all they can from you, and then go and leech off other companies', says one managing director of a family firm. Closely linked to that attitude is 'We can't afford it and even if we could, we could do it better ourselves. They don't deserve our money.' Pride, emotion, the need for privacy, and an element of uncertainty as to how the consultant should be managed result in a heady cocktail.

Making effective use of a consultant

So how should the family business approach the appointment and use of an outside consultant? There are some key questions to be answered:

1. In which areas are we not self-sufficient?
2. In which areas are we in need of third party, unbiased advice?
3. In which areas do we feel that we are losing out to our competitors?
4. In which areas are we devoting most of our time and do we feel that other areas of the operation are being neglected?
5. Who are we talking to about the business from outside the business? Do we talk to them or at them?
6. Which members of the family will be in regular contact with such consultants as we might employ?
7. Are these consultants being brought in for advice or merely for support and affirmation of a decision that has already been made?

In the United States there is a considerable network of specialist advisers to family firms. This network has not evolved in Britain; the bulk of advisory work is conducted by accountancy firms. Perhaps such a network does need to be established. Take, for example, the goals of Will McWhinney, president of Enthusion, Inc.:

I provide a service to a group of people trapped in their own past; sometimes my work is performed simply by allowing a long overdue conversation to take place. Sometimes I work with new tools of thinking, making explicit the family interdependencies and having the opportunity to unsnarl petty and grand conflicts. (*New Management*)

McWhinney argues that the family business consultant operates from a different set of skills and training. An effective family business consultant should have an understanding of human development, about how parents and children work together and how one generation passes on to another. This knowledge has to be linked to an understanding of entrepreneurship and how a business evolves and grows. Finally, there has to be a strong element of business consultancy, understanding business needs and then guiding families towards the best advice in, say, technical or financial help. This is a complex task and not one that is necessarily the province of any one professional adviser who may be hired for their skills as an accountant.

The hideous personal and commercial complexities that can arise if something goes wrong may require a specific form of adviser – a psychologist and organisational specialist. One accountant had recently been made a partner in his firm, which had a number of family business clients. In the main, he was advising them on their pension schemes, on how to plan and manage cash flow, on mitigating corporation tax and devising remuneration packages. With one company, he effectively became the financial director.

Trying to get the father to relinquish hold of the business was like murder. We only did it when we got him into a nursing home and he still won't let go of his shares. He started the company, had it through its good years and now it's suffering badly. The problem is often one of delicate balance; the next generation is the one that is going to pay the audit fees but the current one is the generation that has been paying the audit fees for decades.

There are two issues facing the accountant. One is the problem of being dragged into a situation in which he may have little specific training – it is a human relations problem as much as one of shareholding divestment. Secondly, if there is not precisely a clash of interests, the accountant has to know which piper is paying in order to maintain an ongoing fee-earning contract.

Ultimately, of course, many family disputes centre on power and money. There are few professions better equipped to sort out such wrangles than that of the accountant. But that does not remove the need for someone else, better trained in the dynamics of families, to see the broader behavioural truths.

The accountability of the accountant can also be used as a lever by wily old chairmen. As one accountant complained to me: 'Sometimes you don't actually come into contact with the next generation because they are not shareholders in the business at the time and we will be asked to report solely to the chairman or managing director.'

The use of outside managers

The effective use of outside management is one of the most important cultural experiences for the family firm. It is also one of the most difficult unless it is planned correctly and the lines of responsibility are clear to all. Once the need for outside management has been recognised a vital step has been taken, and it is often this step that is the most difficult to take. Thereafter, it is up to the owner(s) of the business to assess each management position that exists or that will need to be created, and to evaluate the abilities of family candidates particularly in relation to the qualities shown by other managers in other companies in the industry.

While it may still be a psychological hurdle for some family firms to appoint a non-family member to the board, the elevation of, say, a works director or marketing director is not really that traumatic a move. Indeed, it may be the only way in which that particular person is retained within the company. The genuine traumas occur when an outsider is appointed to head the firm.

Often, the appointment of outside management is seen as the first stage in the unwinding of family control. This is often the case. If a firm is not performing well – if its dividends are low, if growth is not occurring, if the next generation does not want to participate, if extra funding is required – then these are usually signs that fresh management is called for. If such results are forthcoming in a public company and the reasons for them are not satisfactory, then the shareholders will call for changes to be made at boardroom level. The family shareholders – and the executive management of a family firm – should apply the same criteria to their own house. Perhaps the question to be posed is: 'If I were an investor in this company, would I be calling for change?'

There is a related issue. Not only should the owner-managers analyse their corporate performance in relation to non-family firms; they should also analyse their recruitment of middle management. If the boardroom is, in the words of Professor David Norburn of Imperial College, 'an elephant's graveyard, a mysterious place where people go to die', then that will reflect on the qualities of the middle management. Indeed, one academic has reported that: 'The problem of recruiting inadequate middle management was inseparable from the practice of reserving senior appointments and directorships for family members.' (Cyril Sofer, *The Organisation from Within*, Tavistock, 1961; quoted by Barry, 1975, p. 300)

There are many potential hazards once the decision to introduce outside management has been made. Obviously, there is that of culture. A family firm has a strong defining culture that will be difficult to absorb and difficult to change. Ownership and management, previously bound together in one family, are divided to a greater or lesser degree. In the view of Bernard Barry (1975), the following characteristics are required:

1. A well-defined chain of command to overcome the confusion that is likely to occur between the traditional and rational-legal authority systems.
2. A formal system of roles and procedures.
3. A division of labour based on functional specialisation.
4. Promotion and selection based on objective assessments of competence.
5. Emphasis on role or office rather than personality.

Fine in theory, many will say, but what about the practice? It is never going to be easy. In the case of the small firm, there is the danger that the new management will endeavour to run the business as if it were their own, excited by the potential and flexibility that it can bring. In the case of the more established firm, rituals, status and contacts can obtrude. (As Barry (1975) remarks, 'It will be a rare family member in, say, the sales director's role who will not be very tempted to use his traditional authority to deal with a production problem holding up a customer's order.')

No one likes ceding control, especially once they have held it or when they have been brought up anticipating the holding of it. So the other critical aspect in the appointment of outside management is how it is presented to members of the family who are working for, or who hope to work for, the firm. Some may leave, disappointed. But others, and probably the able ones, can read such appointments as a sign of commitment to growth and professionalisation. If it shakes up expectations and old comforts, outside management may be the healthiest move for a family business to make.

Recruiting outside executives

Where to recruit from? Problems arise here, too. The small or medium-sized family firm may be unwilling or unable to pay the market price for good quality management. This is either a purely financial reason – as high salaries and perks may be difficult to afford – or because, philosophically, it is not the style of company where the owner-manager has always been able to live a comfortable life, with the business as a security. More than one family chairman has told me that 'money is not the important thing' and they can say that because they have the knowledge that they could sell the business if so needed.

There is, though, the more insidious reason that family businesses do not always pay for the best because they wish to retain a feeling of superiority; their knowledge of the business and how it should be run has to remain paramount. They might defer judgement to skilled craftsmen or production managers, but such deference is a limited functional one. Policy-making remains within the family's purlieu. (The firms that appear to me to be the greatest culprits are those run by brothers. I have no statistical evidence, but I would suspect that the family businesses run with the least amount of outside management will be those run by two or three brothers, and will be second or third generation. The father/son relationship, spiced as it is with intergenerational conflict, is much less likely to be complacent.)

One of the chief catalysts for change is an absence of a genuine family successor or the need for an interim head of the firm. The corrective actions that follow can often be to the enduring benefit of the company, provided that both the incumbent and the family understand the responsibilities to each other.

Case study: Beales and the art of keeping the lines of responsibility clear   A good example of the successful management of this process is Beales of Bournemouth. When Nigel Beale joined the family department store business there were six Beales involved. After five years working in retailing outside the firm, he joined as merchandise manager. 'I regret that I didn't spend much time on accountancy', he says, 'but in the mid-sixties accountancy wasn't very nice and was left to the clerks.'

The board was an elderly one and had never had anything but a Beale serving on it. 'It had never been contemplated', says Beale, 'and it was not considered proper for the company secretary to attend meetings. I used to take the minutes. All the Beales had been brought up through the property or merchandising sides of the operation. In 1969 the first outside director was appointed – as financial director.'

Michael Mitchell joined as company secretary in the late 1970s. At that stage the company was buying stores and there was a lot of legal work to do. Mitchell thought that this was part of a structure that would lead him to secretaryships in ever-larger organisations. 'When I came I would have probably thought that within a few years I would be moving on', he says. That was twelve years ago.

Mitchell's arrival coincided with the first occasion within Beales that internal family succession had not been well in place. Nigel Beale had determined that he should not be chairman and chief executive. The running of the operation was to be split. Says Beale:

It was a short and traumatic period. I took on the chairmanship as the previous generation, almost all at once, stepped down. At the same time, we were making a young outsider the chief executive and he was going to run it his way. The culture shock was short-lived. It could have been a disaster as the shareholders viewed him with suspicion. Some took the line that I was abdicating responsibility. But now we have probably got greater shareholder loyalty than ever before.

Mitchell accepted the job with one proviso – that he was not interfered with in his decision-making. And the Beale family shareholders have remained true to that promise. 'The introduction of an outside chief executive can divide the company', says Beale, 'but we have managed to weld it. There are regular informal discussions between Michael and myself. As I don't interfere I think that he consults me rather more than he might have done. He didn't really believe that the family would allow him to get on with it.'

Both staff and shareholders have been won over, despite initial reservations. As Beale observes:

I constantly say to shareholders that return on investment is more important than running a family business and that we are employing 750 people who are entitled to a job and the possibility of promotion. Shareholders were concerned that Michael would trade the company down for short-term sales. They asked whether he would abandon our traditional standards of customer service. And it can be hard to explain to a 75-year-old Lieutenant-Colonel that department stores are not going to pay his dividends by just remaining old-fashioned department stores.

A lot of staff have been with us a long time and it is difficult for them to adjust to not having a Mr Beale as boss. They are tempted to take me on one side and ask that things are changed back to the old ways. So you have to maintain an aura but dissociate yourself from decisions. There are still plenty of people who think that I personally own the business.

This does rub off. I just have to bite my tongue and talk to Michael about it. But it is difficult after many years of being able to do what I wanted.

In Beales' case, a crucial decision was taken to split the roles of chairman and chief executive. Beale is an executive chairman, Mitchell the chief executive. External affairs and customer liaison are very much Beale's province, as is shareholder communication. He holds a relatively high profile, working hard also for the Association of Independent Stores, a trade body. Meanwhile, Mitchell concentrates on business development and the recruitment of new management. 'It's now a family business not entirely run by the family', Beale comments. 'It's helpful, but not critical, to have a family member on the board. The customer feels comfortable. But it's quite wrong to canvass the family to come in.'

The lines of responsibility are clear, even though some of the older staff would like to think otherwise. A new pattern has been set, one that not so long ago was nearly unthinkable. It was brought about by a recognition of the family's own limitations and the need for outside, professional management. The company's performance has improved and looks set to continue, with new ventures in franchising and sports equipment as well as acquisitions in funeral directing, another service business run by plenty of family firms.

Mitchell enjoys an autonomy as chief executive. At the same time he has bought a reasonable shareholding in the company. He can thus stand apart from the family interests and yet be integrated with the long-term goals of independence and profitability. This is a balance that has to be found. If it is not, then the relationship can suffer.

One company that I met had had to appoint a non-executive chairman following the retirement of the father. The appointee was someone who had the backing of an investing institution. The relationship failed; the family felt that the chairman had the institution's interest too much at heart and the family was not controlling the destiny of the company. The goals of the family and the chairman were too far apart.

The process need not be inevitable, but there are some clear morals to be drawn. The outside manager, if he is to be effective, has to be integrated into the culture of the company. He must also have incentives and those incentives will probably include a stake in the business. He must have a clear understanding of the lines of responsibility and accountability and the family must stick to those lines. If growth is an objective of the family business, then there will come a time when, despite all the qualities of the family, they will not be enough to manage growth successfully. That is when outside management is needed. But if the resources of outside management are to be harnessed successfully, it may necessitate some change in the way that the family thinks and how it apportions reward. For, unlike the employment of consultants, or even non-executives, the hiring of outside managers is the hiring of someone who is risking a job and a salary – they are not in the business of giving favours on the cheap.

The use of non-executive directors

The non-executive director is an essential prerequisite in the family business. Increasingly, all manner of firms are taking on non-executive directors to provide them with a helpful, experienced view that is outside the day-to-day running – and problems – of the business. The non-executive director acts as an adviser, a source of contacts and an arbiter.

The non-executive should, in essence, be a captive consultant – available, knowledgeable and not financially tied to the firm. There are few family firms which could say in all honesty that they are not in need of such a person. The trick comes in choosing the right person.

'The best way of making sure that the independent voice is heeded in a family firm is for it to appoint independent, outside directors to its board', says Sir Adrian Cadbury. 'Outsiders will help to ensure that the board acts as a board, rather than as a management committee, and a board provides a structure through which non-family directors can exercise influence over the policies and plans of the firm.'

Non-executives: stories from the front

'The non-executive should be an informed, financially disinterested sounding-board', says John Cheele, who acts as a non-executive for a family business. 'Just by talking they get a blinding flash of the bloody obvious.'

Cheele's own experience gives him a good qualification to speak on the subject. He started off in a family business – 'I never actually applied for a job' – after doing his national service. He joined a part of it where the challenge was to make it work: 'It was a case of sink or swim', he recalls. In 1972 his mother died and three years later the company was sold to a larger PLC. 'That was okay', says Cheele, 'and I became chief executive until 1987. Then the PLC management said "thanks and goodbye".'

He took up an offer from a friend to be a non-executive of his family business and discovered that he enjoyed the role. 'I liked the non-executive position and I realised that I had been blinkered by the family business. I had had no outside experience. I find the position stimulating. I'm 52 now and am learning to modify the old tricks.' He now sits as a non-executive on a number of other small companies, most of them family firms.

So too does Laurence Hill, formerly managing director of the retail stores department of BAT Industries (BAT). In his view, the problem of family businesses is that 'They don't work out where either the people or the business want to be in, say, ten years' time. They have to watch out in case they become too insular, and that is an important function for the non-executive director.'

In one instance, Hill put into place an appraisal system and a mission statement within a family firm. They have been effective, he believes, as they ask simple but basic questions: What are we about? What are we seeking to achieve? He acknowledges the hurdles; to some family firms, suggestions such as these imply criticism.

The arguments for non-executive directors do seem to be prevailing. Regular analysis and reports of their effectiveness always help. Take, for example, a £15 million family business in the north-west. It was founded by the chairman's great-grandfather in the late nineteenth century, bringing in wines and selling them straight to the consumer through its own retail outlets. Initially it started with one outlet and bottling occurred in the cellar; now it has forty outlets and is looking to expand. It has always been an independent family firm.

The board used to be entirely family members, split between executive and non-executive directors. Now the non-executives are split equally between family and non-family members.

Growth is continuing and has been especially fast in the past five years. The main business is its retailing interest but a recent acquisition has extended its interests in drinks packaging and bottling. Says the current chairman:

Our family non-executives are both approaching retirement age. We have wanted – or I have wanted – to strengthen the board. Non-executive directors are important; being a family business we need outside comment, guidance and contribution. We need someone outside the wood, so to speak. They will ask questions – why are we doing this? The family tends to say 'That's alright by us. You seem to be doing alright.' And they just let you go more or less. Nobody tends to jolt you, or bring you up. But that needs to be done. We were looking for someone who had been involved in marketing and retailing and who had a strong accountancy background, and certainly more knowledge of high finance than we were used to.

Initially the company looked at people who were personally known to members of the board. There were some possible candidates but 'The chemistry was not right.' Having exhausted this list, the company went to the Institute of Directors. Out of a list of five qualified candidates they were able to choose one.

Their eventual choice was a man who was clear in his understanding as to what the company wanted and who felt a confidence in the chemistry:

They were looking for business experience, someone who could sit slightly apart from it, who could be objective and who understood the business. They wanted someone to provide areas of back-up where they were not so strong; for example, I had had computer departments reporting to me. I'm no computer expert but I had had some useful commercial experience in this area. There's no great mystique to any of this. It's just a matter of asking questions; why are you doing it like this? And 90 per cent of it is common sense. Executive directors can often take a lot of things for granted.

You may also have conflicting views among executives. There may well be organisational change which affects the executives who will all have vested interests. It may be setting right something that has gone wrong, particularly in people-related issues. Have you got the right people in place?

And, as the speaker points out, vested interests have as large a place in a family firm as they do in, say, a lucrative management buy-out. The non-executive describes further his role in this north-west company:

If this was a public company you would have read about an impressive growth record with a rapid improvement in profitability. You would be a go-go stock. Now, if you require substantial financial resources as a family business you will be faced with a dilution of equity. Where do you get the finance? Will the family remain in control? As a family business, you are in control of that expansion and what you require from that expansion may not be flotation. So that expansion has to be controlled. It can be very different from a public company.

As a non-executive director you act as an objective observer. For the family some of the messages you deliver may not be very palatable. Take retailing. A lot of retail operations are driven by strong entrepreneurs. How do you tell them that their ideas are now five years out of date? They have had fantastic success and they grow up with it but that success may just be associated with the previous decade. The same thing can happen with families. This was where I was very careful about this appointment. Here I think you can see a family who want to take the thing forward but who are still living with what created their success some years ago rather than what is necessary to compete in the market-place today and be successful. They aren't necessarily the same thing. Non-executive directors are the people to talk these things through with but it's very difficult with families because they have lived with the business and have strong affinities with it. The non-executive does not have a strong affinity with what initially created the success. What impressed me about this family business was that they are determined to take it forward, that they were open-minded and were not wedded to the past.

The non-executive director is assisting the firm in the implementation of a financial strategy. The family chairman recognises the need for this:

Obviously, we would like to retain family control and remain independent. It is something that I believe firmly matters a lot to the employees. I get asked now more than ever: 'Are you going to stay in the family business? Are you going to sell?' and it really matters to them. It all depends: yes, it would be nice but can we maintain the growth as a family business? That is constantly a question in our minds. We are looking to our non-executive directors for their expertise. For example, our borrowings are very low but he has had experience of running a company with very high borrowings. That knowledge will come through. Our finances are pretty sound now but there will be a time when we ask: What do we do? We shall have to find some extra finance at some stage.

The business will need projections. It needs to know where the critical decision points lie in the future and it needs to discuss them now, if only so that it can expand as far as it can without conceding financial control. Apart from such specific advice, the chairman benefits from the challenge that an outsider brings:

I have been on the board for a considerable time. There was a time when only the family sat on the board. Those were passive meetings.

No one asked any questions because everyone was in fear of rocking the boat to some degree. As the chairman, I need outside influence. I believe that to go the way we want to go we have got to have somebody asking us questions. They don't necessarily always have to be difficult questions, but questions about the way we are thinking, the way we lay things out, the way we want things to go. And it's a very good way of making things clear in your own mind. Our non-executive's questions are not uncomfortable, but we have had input that wasn't there before. His questions spark conversations which didn't happen before. Occasionally those questions should be uncomfortable but their real job is to start a discussion.

As chairman, I find it very difficult to talk to family non-executive directors who really haven't got the expertise that I want. One is an engineer and the other is a solicitor. Yet for legal advice I would use the company solicitors.

One of the things that we had not done properly before was structuring ourselves correctly. We have now done it but we could have done it earlier had we thought about it. If our non-executive had been on the board a couple of years ago, I'm sure that the questions would have been asked. Before, we were working hard, improving our profits and performance, and then suddenly there was this problem to be sorted out. Someone outside would have seen it coming earlier than we did.

Non-executives in established family businesses

It seems as if many more family businesses are taking the role of the non-executive more seriously. Even established, resolutely family-only fourth and fifth generation firms are contemplating the shift. One chairman said to me:

Non-executives? Well, yes but not quite. We have a marketing consultant who has taken on the title of head of marketing and he will attend the board meetings that discuss sales and marketing. He won't attend the whole board meeting but we see it as a half-way house to a non-executive post. It's a significant move; it's not happened here before. But the question of non-executives does raise its head regularly. We're going to see how this goes and if the idea seems to be to the benefit of the company then we can develop it from there.

Questions for discussion

Objectivity at a decision-making level is clearly an important role for the non-executive director, but it is not the only one. The non-executive can also pose important questions that help to clarify priorities. Non-executive John Cheele has a set of questions upon which to base initial discussions with family firms:

I ask them to separate themselves into their separate roles – the executive, the company director and the part-owner of the business. They have to understand this tripartite role and they have to be separated. It is a very difficult thing to do. Often, heads of family firms see themselves as entities who go from home to the office and run the business; the differences between being an owner and a director are rarely considered, but they are considerable ones. Nobody told me about that when I was running our family business and I wish now that they had – I'm sure that my performance would have been better.

You have got to take the individual out of the business. You need to take them out for a pint and make them think. As an owner, are you a perpetual owner? Are you handing down the company as of right or as a duty? Would you accept an offer for the company? What are your plans for the future?

Yet directorship has nothing to do with ownership. You may have non-shareholding directors who share these responsibilities with you. The duties and obligations upon all of you as directors are very different to the issues and problems that you face as an owner.

This view is also asserted by Bernard Barry. 'As family members in a business usually occupy three roles simultaneously (for example, as family members they are responsible for the family's investment; as directors they are concerned with the future of the firm; and, as managers, they have departmental interests) the potential for role conflict is obvious.' (Barry, 1975, p. 302)

Cheele says that he has talked to a number of family firms about this issue. Their receptiveness, he notes, tends to be linked to the size of the enterprise. The smaller the business, the harder the concept is to understand. Battles are having to be fought there and then and there is no time to distance the owner from the business; the larger companies, with more executives, can find more time to talk about these matters.

The issue of succession is another aspect of family business management where the non-executive can play a vital role. It should be part of the non-executive's armoury of first questions: Who does what? Where do individual family members come from and what is their experience? What planning has been made for succession?

It is the non-executive director who can often postulate the unthinkable: What happens if the intended successor dies early, or decides not to want the job? It is also the non-executive who can inch forward those often-painful discussions (or non-discussions) between father and son. Non-executives should always see this role – the negotiator between parents and children – as a necessary part of their job. (If it transpires not to be needed, then that is a luxury!)

'Non-executives can get sons and fathers talking together', says John Cheele. 'Almost by definition fathers are too negative about their sons or are too far towards the positive. Nobody seems to get it right. It may be better to be negative under most circumstances. I think that's increasingly the case.'

Cheele has yet to be asked, in his capacity as non-executive, to make a judgement upon the son. 'The emotions that are in play then are rather like giving your children a car after they have passed their driving test. Parents do find it difficult to recognise their children's skills and abilities.'

The demands made upon the non-executive are almost as hard as those placed upon the family executives. Non-executives need to postulate in public and in private all the crises that a family business can face. Yet they are not a universal panacea, as their advice only works when it is integrated with a sense of executive purpose, and sometimes that can be too strong. One non-executive told me this particular story.

A manufacturing company, successful in its field, was handed on from father to son. The father had been an inspirational figure, big in presence as well as in drive. He was a man who believed in management-by-walking-about and his workforce admired him the more for that. His son, though, was both quieter in nature and shorter in stature. The workforce did not hold him in the same regard, although he practised an open-door policy. Outsiders sensed that an ivory tower was being built and became disaffected. The board recognised the problem and appointed three non-executives. But some could not take the management style – there was little interaction between the shop-floor and the boardroom. Indeed, when a non-executive walked around the plant there was surprise at his being there. A call for an outside chief executive was motioned by the non-executives but was not passed. Some non-executives resigned. Eventually, the firm was bid for and won by an industrial conglomerate, even though the family had held over 30 per cent of the business.

When the non-executive must challenge

The non-executive will be a boon to a family business only if the business is prepared to use him as a sounding-board and a challenger, rather than as a phantom or an echo. Indeed, the same questions that a family asks when it is considering the introduction of an executive director from outside the family should be asked of a non-executive, although they should be asked not in terms of dilemma-solving but as a guide to recognising just exactly who it is that they are looking for.

Such questions might include the following:

1. In which areas do we lack skills and abilities?
2. How will they relate to family directors?
3. What impact will they have on the family non-executives?
4. What role will they expect to play and what role do we expect them to play?
5. How should we choose them?

Another particular area in which the non-executive could have a distinct role to play, possibly in conjunction with the firm's accountant, is over the question of remuneration. Non-family non-executives, with a wide remit to gather information, can then form a remuneration committee. Just as not all managers are paid equally but may be paid on performance, so too can executive directors be judged. It is a proposal that may not find much favour among many family businesses but it may well be something to consider before appointing a non-executive. As one non-executive put it to me:

The rigours of the audit are increasing and the exploitation of limited companies by some executive owners is out of step with this increasing rigour. Take, for example, the second generation chairman whose wife's car is funded by the company. The potential exists for such practices to be deemed 'unclean'. The auditors may require 'a presence in the court' to monitor such affairs – and that presence will be a non-executive director from outside the family.

The advent of the non-family non-executive is both a challenge and an opportunity for the family business. Before they are introduced, the family must clarify a lot of issues in its own mind as it will need to be able to communicate its values and ways of working to the non-executive. It must also brace itself for some probing questions and some challenges to previously unchallenged assumptions.

The family member as a non-executive director

Perhaps one of the major assumptions that it will have to face is the role of the family member as a non-executive member of the board. The appointment of family non-executives is often regarded as a useful way out of argument; it is a fair compromise to have somebody, who has a stake in the company, represented without complicating the executive structure. It is a move that at best is harmless to the point of passivity, and at worst is a storehouse of trouble that could lead to the demise of the company's independence.

The family non-executive is a potential disaster. Even the outgoing chairman, who has managed an efficient transition of power, should be shunted off the board and retained only as a consultant.

There are many reasons for my dogmatic stance. The family non-executive is a contradiction in terms. The non-executive is appointed on the grounds of independence; the family member is not independent. The non-executive should have only a minute shareholding in the company, if any at all; the family member may have the vested interest of a stake – and often a considerable one – in the company. A family non-executive with little or no stake in the company is likely to treat the job as a sinecure; a family non-executive with a large stake will attempt to influence decision-making in such a way as to enhance their returns. (What happens if an offer is made for the company? The executives will be more likely to wish to remain independent while a non-executive, replete with privileged information, is more likely to recommend a sale.) The family non-executive is likely to represent the high-dividend, low-investment approach, even at times when different paths are vitally needed. Each member of the board has to be there because they bring skills and abilities; a family non-executive is more often than not serving that position because of blood.

There may be howls of protest from many honest, upright, disinterested family members serving as non-executives on the family business – I am sure there are many such around. But the truth is that they will rarely challenge in the effective way that a genuine outsider can. The family non-executive is truly a hangover from dynasticism; unless every family firm sets about their replacement, many more will continue to struggle rather than prosper.

The appointment of non-executives from outside gives the management a chance to reassess the business. The non-executives bring fresh eyes to problems and a fresh view on to the perspectives and the values held by the family in the running of the firm. They provide the opportunity (sometimes even the excuse) to eliminate old ways and means while retaining strengths. They provide the opportunity for introducing new thinking that will help the firm adapt. Family non-executives are unlikely to do this; indeed, they are more likely to promote stasis, to hark back.

7   Training the new generation

In comparison to the United States, there is little management development and training in the United Kingdom that dedicates itself to the family firm. True, some would argue that although more MBA courses and the like are available than in Germany, they have not provided a strength and depth of management competence. Indeed, the effect may have been the reverse – in that the pursuit of the MBA has distracted resources, able people and time away from practical apprenticeship.

This is not the appropriate place for such discussion. What is clear, however, is that the new generation entering today's family firm faces some clear choices and must press for changes in the way academic establishments treat the family firm.

The apprentice route

Traditionally, the family firm has been a practical grounding for young members of the family. As soon as he wants to – and often as soon as his parents want him to – the first son is introduced to the shop-floor. He will learn about the business from the bottom up, from cleaning the floors and generally tidying up the mess of the working day. The chances are that he may earn his pocket money from doing so.

Gradually, as he grows up, he is given less menial chores to do. He will learn from the various foremen, craftsmen and supervisors what to do in each department. He may find that there is one area that interests him in particular and he may be allowed to revert to that job with each school holiday. On the other hand, his father may have more structured ideas in mind and will deliberately place him in different departments each time.

There is little harm in this. The father's firm is seen as a natural place to work during school holidays, particularly if it pays pocket money. The son is treated reasonably well by most of the employees; he occupies, after all, a privileged position as the son of the boss. If he shows an aptitude, then it is encouraged and pleasure in his progress and his interest will be shown by both the parents and the workforce. A warmth and a security are shared by father and son.

What occurs in those teenage years is the assimilation of the company culture and also a bonding process. Each time the son returns to the firm, he is absorbed a stage further. The workforce begins to expect to see him; the father expects the son to participate; the son begins to see it as the natural sequence of events. Plans are made further in advance. Instead of 'seeing what can be done' at school holiday time, the father examines what his son has done so far and what he should 'try to get him to do this time'. The process is one of osmosis. It is, in effect, an informal apprenticeship that is being served.

There are clear advantages and disadvantages of this process. In businesses where defined skills are required, it ensures that the future managing director – if that is what the son eventually transpires to be – has a clear understanding of each stage of the manufacturing process. It means that he can talk to his technical director or his production manager with authority and understanding. In many instances, it leads to a passionate commitment to quality and a willingness to experiment and innovate.

On the other hand, the ex-apprentice can suffer from myopia, brought on by being too close to the product for too long. The end product, and the means by which it has been produced, is not the only concern. But it can look that way. The association may be made between 'the product' and 'the family' with little consideration given to the ever-increasing number of complex external pressures that are brought to bear upon the smallest company.

Then there is the attitude of the workforce. The son who has been involved in all aspects of the operation can earn respect – if he has done the job at all well. He will be seen as reasonably suitable for the future running of the company because he has been tried, tested and proven. Yet it has to be conducted at all levels and departments. A failure in, say, the finance or sales department can get brushed under the carpet of overall management development. While the workforce and the father must recognise that everybody has their strengths and their weaknesses, it is both dangerous and impossible to ignore shortcomings in a putative successor. If the son shows particular abilities in one field, it is important that they are not pandered to at an early stage. Otherwise, weaknesses will not be addressed and overcome.

Clearly, the osmotic process breeds both a loyalty to the firm and also a spirit of healthy enquiry as to how it is faring. Conversation about trivial and important issues continues beyond the bounds of the workplace; home is not just where one lives, it is an extension of the workplace. The firm with its culture, its objectives and its problems gets into the blood.

'When you see your father coming back from work, talking about it, it intrigues you', says the managing director of one fifth generation business. 'My father came home with problems and I began to see it as a challenge. It does run in the blood.'

This view was particularly noticeable when I was talking to established family firms, representing perhaps three generations at any one time and with numerous scions of the family within the organisation. In these instances, the organisation is often strong enough to insist that family members have to achieve some qualification outside before they join the business. Here, there is no desperation to make the business attractive to the individual son or daughter.

'There is a tradition at work', says Michael Passmore, chairman of Passmore International, one of the larger family printing concerns in the country. 'The family has done it for so long that it becomes more of a challenge than a sinecure.'

Insisting on qualifications

Passmore says that 'If I had any sort of views on the family joining the business – and I think that it's true of most family businesses – it's that no member of the family should come in without a qualification'. He adds:

Now, if you ask me 'what qualification?' I would find that hard to answer but I think that the logic behind it is that if you want to fall out, you can. You then have a qualification to fall back on and you are in the position of being able to earn a reasonable living without being dependent on being in the company. If something should happen to the company or if you wanted to disagree, you should be in a position to stand on your own two feet and say 'I'm capable and not dependent on anyone.'

And, in practice, the Passmores operate like this. Michael's daughter, Stella, trained to go into the hotel business. Afterwards, she made her decision to apply to join the family business.

Why did I join? Well, I wasn't encouraged by my father. There seemed to be a time when it just fitted, and the job that I do [production manager] involves similar skills to those that I learned in the hotel trade. However, if we were a firm of accountants I don't think that I would have joined! It didn't come up as a topic of conversation whether I would join. You do what you think is the right thing at the right time.

The Passmores are convinced of the need to do another job first. 'It is difficult to say to an 18-year-old Passmore "We want you to do this." First of all, they need to show that they have the ability and the commitment to come into the company', says Nigel Passmore, sales and marketing director.

Stella worked in the production office for a couple of years and then went to Australia. On her return she worked as a print buyer in London.

There is a lot of pressure being a family member. I think that you are suspect. You ask yourself questions: 'Am I right for the job? Do they really want me in there? Am I just family? I got a lot more confident by working for other people. In the family business you do think that people are looking at you twice and are analysing you more. I needed to get out and find for myself that I was worthy of the job.

Her cousin Nigel agrees. 'It's difficult to say what qualification you need except that a professional qualification in some area of management. I have an HND in business studies from the London College of Printing.'

I was always keen, apart from a brief spell of wanting to be a journalist, to get into this business. I thought that I could find other ways around the problems that my father faced. But I was never pushed into it at all. In many ways, my parents said 'Go and do something else.' That in itself does create a challenge, as I then wanted all the more to get into this and prove myself.

The most recent example of a Passmore recruitment is that of Chris, Michael Passmore's eldest son, who was in the Royal Navy until the age of 30. 'He came to a crossroads', explains Nigel. 'We actively encouraged him to come into the business because he had a lot of qualifications and was a sound young man. But, and I must emphasise this, we put him through all the interview procedures and he reports to me on the sales side. In the same way that Michael does a regular performance appraisal with me, I do with Chris. He has sales targets to achieve.'

The company has developed an admission procedure. But it has, admits Michael Passmore, been one that has been developed by experience. Both he and Nigel admit to weaknesses in the procedure only five years ago. Now they believe they have a more professional approach. 'It's because of competitive pressures and the demands they place on the organisation. We can't afford to carry people', says Nigel.

Michael recalls another family printing business – Donnelly's in the United States. 'Mrs Donnelly has a slogan', he says. 'It is "Just remember, you are there to serve the company, not the company to serve you". That's an important concept of which I think we are all now aware. The ethos has got to be that of serving the company. Nobody owes you a living.'

Passmore conducts two staff appraisals per year. Says Michael:

It has not developed as much as it should have done, although it has not been in operation long. I think, however, that it is right. It sets out the structure; what people are meant to be doing, how it's done and achieved, where you fit into the picture, who you have to communicate with. It's a very important thing.

What is important is that standard corporate practices are being observed. The company is big enough and diverse enough to attract family members in the way it attracts non-family members. It is also big enough to put them through the same hoops.

Not every family firm has the same options. Indeed, it is probably a privileged few who reach the stage that the Passmores have. There is another family business that I have seen where the managing director actually employed headhunting techniques in order to persuade a niece to leave a good job in the City and

join the family concern! For many others, the choice was stark
or unconsidered.

Learning by luck

'I joined because I thought it was the easy way out', says one
chairman of a small London family owned business.

I left school with a number of O and A levels and I wasn't sure what I
wanted to do. The only thing I was certain about was that I didn't want
to do anything. I felt that my Dad had looked after me successfully for
seventeen years so I didn't see why he couldn't carry on for another
few months. He fell in with that for a while. Then he made it pretty
plain that I had to make up my own mind. Eventually I decided to
join him. It seemed to be a good idea and there was money in it – so
why not?

Three months after school I was packing parcels which wasn't quite
my idea of what I was going to be doing! I was going to be running the
thing from Day One and it turned out to be a lot harder than I thought
it was going to be. The problem is an emotional one. When you start out
working with your father you have a view of your relationship which is
totally different from the reality of working with him. He was bloody
tough. He was really hard. And, it turned out that he was right. I learned
to work each of the machines in the building. I was forced through a
regimen of knowing everything about every single job. It stood me in
good stead.

If you work for your father your rise is fast. In some cases it is meteoric.
You are viewed, though, as your father's son and not as somebody who
has come in to run a business. So you have to overcome that. That's
the handicap, overcoming people's natural suspicions. And, of course,
initially the only reason that you are there is precisely because you are
your father's son. You have to work twice as hard to prove that you
can do it. There is a massive advantage of walking into a ready-made
situation; it is easier starting from something that is already there. You
face two battles: learning to progress yourself and convincing everybody
else that you are capable of doing it.

My father had mixed views about my joining the company. Part of him
said 'great, nice if the business continues', but he would have liked me to
have gone away and learned something else first and had some sort of
qualification. But I was fed up with learning at that stage of my life. I had
spent most of my last year organising amateur dramatics and father had
not been particularly overjoyed. He liked the plays but it wasn't really
what he had in mind for me. My younger brother is a solicitor. That's
probably partly because he couldn't stand working with me and partly
because there was some pressure from my parents for him to get that
qualification.

In the early stages, I thought that I knew it all and that my father was an old fool. That's bad enough in your normal development but it's worse when you are actually working for him. The early days were hard. There was someone who had built a business and had definite views as to how it should be run. Those views don't always coincide with some kid like me saying 'This is how we should do it' with all the certainty that no experience at all tends to bring.

Are there things that I would do differently? I would have listened more, for sure. I suppose that as soon as I joined the objective was to groom me to take over. But you can't put a finger on the exact date that it was made apparent. My father came in one day and said that he was going to retire. All we said was 'oh, yes?' and carried on without paying attention to him at all. And he proceeded to do what he had been doing. It was a gradual process of my taking on more and more responsibility while he performed the difficult task of standing back and watching me make mistakes without interfering too much. If you don't make mistakes, you don't learn either. If he had thought a mistake was going to be absolutely disastrous he would have stopped it. It is the best way of learning. And, of course, in turn, when you are running it, it is difficult to let anyone else do it because you can't sit still and watch somebody do something that you know is wrong.

You always think that you can do it. It's quite embarrassing when you think of the things that you might have said and done. It was very gradual. It wasn't a case of me pushing all the time. I drifted into it. In reality, the business was earning good money for everybody; it was always in credit and it was a comfortable existence. I had been insulated pretty well. It was the wrong environment for thrusting.

Getting recruitment right

The permutations are endless. It is clear that there are some lessons to be drawn. The recruitment, training and development of family members within the family business are not usually structured. Yet it is the area that could ultimately lead to successful succession and transition if enough time is devoted to it.

Families do not employ the same criteria for judgement that a company does. The two must not be confused in the minds of either generation. In a company, objectives can be set. If they are not, there will be – or at least there should be – rational, logical discussion as to why they were not. This is not the stuff of the conversation of uncle and cousin, or father and daughter, in the comfortable domestic setting of home. But it has to be in the workplace and it has to be understood from the outset. The danger of drifting into the company, having worked with it as a teenager, is that these lines of demarcation are not fully expressed. It would be interesting to know just how many family firms could point to performance contracts signed by members of the family.

The fact is that recruitment of one member of the family usually rests with another member of the family. The question of whether or not to employ a relative invites something of a Hobson's choice. 'If he recruits an incompetent relative he gets trouble in the business. If he does not recruit the relative he gets trouble in the family. A similar dilemma is faced when considering firing an incompetent relative.' (Stoy Hayward, 1989, p. 30)

Training is another issue that is raised here. 'Should family members be trained according to what is best for the individuals (the family norm) or according to what is best for the business? Unfortunately, the two rarely coincide.' (Stoy Hayward, 1989, p. 29)

For the smaller firm, the best advice would appear to be that any prospective successor should be encouraged – forced, perhaps – to spend at least four years away from the business. Only in this way can they obtain experience that is not clouded by the son of the boss syndrome, and which provides them with a distance from the business from which they can view it objectively. A dominating father – and many entrepreneurs are – is not a healthy single source of wisdom and advice.

From a management perspective, relatives should be treated in the same way as others when seeking employment; give them a job only if they possess the right skills. From an ownership perspective, relatives interested in working for the firm should be given the opportunity to acquire the necessary skills, but the funds should be provided by the family, not by the firm. If relatives acquire the appropriate skills and become competent enough, then they can be employed. Thus, relatives are treated in accordance with family norms without compromising the firm's standards. (Stoy Hayward, 1989, p. 31)

Blood being thicker than water can cloud perceptions. This is particularly true of abilities. Ineptitude is easily masked over. The recruiter should have a slogan, a phrase, in his or her mind when contemplating a relative in the firm. 'Are they up to the job?' is not an elegant phrase but it suits the purpose. 'Why am I employing him or her?' is equally brutal but it demands an answer. Perhaps a simple exercise can be drawn up: mask out the names from a number of curricula vitae and send them to a headhunter along with a job description. Then defend your decision. (This assumes, however, that others were considered for the job. In most cases, this is unlikely to be so).

The need for rigorous reporting

No matter how small the operation, the reporting system for the family member has to be rigorous. The careful line that has to be drawn is between being over-rigorous, where excessive zeal in discipline and goal-setting can rebound, persuading the relative to leave for a job where the pressures are not so artificially great, and being too lax, where it can be perceived as a sham by other employees. Ideally, it should be conducted by peers and senior non-family executives and should take the form of an appraisal, assessing the quality of the contribution made to the firm and the development potential. It would be unwise to incorporate relatives into this group on a day-to-day basis, as complaints and embarrassments and arguments are usually best discussed away from the most sensitive ears at the initial stage.

In many ways, the problems faced by family members is a reverse of that faced by those who join non-family firms. We want to make progress up and through an organisation but there are no clear signposts as to how long that will take. There is a top job – or a number of senior jobs – to which we might aspire. If we cannot achieve these goals within that organisation, we can move on. For the member of the family firm, the responsibility of the top job – or of a senior job – can be cast as a mantle at the very outset. They have a clearer idea as to how long it will take, determined by their father's age. It is not a question of 'if' they do but rather of 'whether' they can achieve the goals set for them by others. There is less flexibility; the chance of free movement is curtailed.

Setting up reporting procedures

It is bearing this in mind that a reporting procedure needs to be set up. Both family and non-family need to be clear and decided about what it is they are trying to learn and what are the best ways of judging the results. If there is a dispute at this stage, it should be determined by outside advice.

The very action of creating a reporting procedure is a healthy exercise. It brings family members back to the basic question: What are the goals of the family and what are the goals of the company?

To what extent are these goals complementary or opposed? How are these issues perceived or understood by others in the firm? Is there a consensus between the family and the senior managers?

To many family firms this will smack of excessive formalisation. Informality is an abiding allure to many. It is one of the strengths of the family firm; it is one of the qualities that differentiates a family business from an impersonal one.

Yet the family business cannot hold on to all the cherished ideals of informality. Training and development, to be effective, requires careful programmes, schedules and tests. These might run counter to the culture of the firm. For the family firm to succeed, for it to offer adequate training and development so as to groom the best possible successor, patterns of formalisation are required.

The new generation and the MBA

Nowhere is this more apparent than in attitudes towards the MBA. Here is a profound cultural divide between fathers and their children. It is one that will test the family firm.

Clive Cutler recently completed an MBA course at Ashridge. His father's company, Pearce & Cutler, has a turnover of £20 million and is divided into three autonomous units. He is confident that the course has been of great benefit. 'It gave me a distance. When you are too close to a family business, you don't always see a strategic plan for it', he says.

The course that Cutler attended is a recent one, devised in the main by Laurence Handy. He says that he has had a fair proportion of applicants coming from family firms.

The Ashridge example

'Our programme was designed for managerial succession and it just so happens that it's quite good for small family businesses', he says, 'as it involves work on a project that will be useful for the development of the business. Students have to produce a substantial piece of work that should be relevant to their own business; it rounds them and gets them to understand their work. When they go back they are forced to communicate with their employees or their family. I believe it cements the relationship between them.'

Handy describes the Ashridge MBA as being driven by a philosophy of learning by doing. Students are forced to ask and answer the questions as to whether it is relevant. 'They are tailoring it themselves', he says.

The course is one of Handy's own devising and the first programme ran in 1988.

I had a clean sheet of paper. It was intended for more mature students who wouldn't learn by sitting on their backsides. The evidence that we have had confirms our approach; mature people learn by their own experiences, from the people they meet and from the challenge. Our MBA is based on the ways that managers learn.

Handy and his staff identify with the candidate the new areas that they can learn about. So, for instance, a candidate from a family firm may have had no experience of working for, or with, large companies and may have held only a handful of functional management positions but is being groomed for chairmanship. So the project would seek to link him or her up with a large firm related to his or her own industry, where he or she can learn about competition on a global scale, about the pressures being placed upon small suppliers and the reasons for those pressures, about the changing face of future markets. The whole intent and purpose is to broaden the candidate's experience. It also enables the candidate to meet people from large companies and make useful contacts (useful, that is, if his or her own company was to expand.)

In Handy's course, the choice is between a one-year or two-year programme. Little change will be received from £16,500. Says Handy:

We interview anyone who looks credible. And it is not just the individual, but also the company. The client for the project is the chief executive and that fact puts the necks of the students on to the chopping block. What I ask the company for is a sheet of paper that outlines what they are looking to get out of it, what they regard as the key result areas. So the candidate has an idea of what they are attempting to do. It's not a Ph.D., it's a consultancy project with regular meetings and boardroom briefings. It's a real piece of work. I haven't had a project that has failed and I don't expect one to do so.

The project, which amounts to two-thirds of the total MBA is assessed at four stages (described by Handy as 'definition, design, the interim report and the preliminary to the final report'). Each stage goes to the board of the company involved. (The other aspects of the course include assignments that are tested by examination, such as financial analysis.)

'Half or more of the time on the Ashridge MBA is active, practical learning and application', claims Handy. 'It acts like a funnel; you put a lot in to start with and you end up with a concentrated cup of coffee at the end.'

He says that there are several types of prospective graduates who are applying. Large companies will select candidates themselves. Individuals may send in a CV based on an assurance of support from a company. (Most such approaches come to fruition.) There are those who apply as a basis upon which to change jobs. ('I'm sympathetic but they have to find a company to do a project for', says Handy.) Some are looking to set up their own businesses but want an MBA in order to gain additional experience. Then there are small business owners who have sold up and who want to gain big business experience. 'I am really quite surprised at the number of small organisations that have been interested', says Handy. 'I am getting a lot of 23- and 24-year old sons and daughters but I think that they are too young. I tend to offer counsel and delay.'

Companies, Handy believes, have not thought sufficiently about what they will do with the returning candidates:

The reasons that many will have for sending a candidate to us are often highly political. Some, say, want an MBA in order to give a member of the firm a bit more credibility in the City. But that is not what I am driven by. We are in a development programme, demanding proof of competence in their work.

So does the MBA carry a talismanic quality? Handy thinks that to some extent it does:

The self-made businessman often has no qualifications but he will say that he wants to invest in his sons and daughters. If you have the money, then you put it into an education process that you did not yourself go through. But it can also be equally practical. If the proprietor and his children are genuinely interested in the business, then you will find that the proprietor has woken up to the fact that his son is, say, 25 and that he is not going to go on forever.

If that is the case, we have to ask whether the MBA will give the new generation the benefits and advantages that they seek. We must also ask whether there is a succession problem within that company. We ask what experience has the son or daughter had so far. Often the answer is 'not much'. So the MBA gives the son of the boss an internal credibility. But that internal credibility must be developed within the company rather than just from the outside. Then there is the external credibility; if a family business wants some external investor, then an MBA shows that the calibre of management is there. But that is only part, rather than the whole, of the story.

A Cranfield example

MBAs are now the trend for the next generation of family firms but they are still a drop in the ocean', says Professor Sue Birley, professor of entrepreneurship at Imperial College, London, 'as they cannot be separated from the whole culture'. In her previous position at the Cranfield School of Management, she says that more than you would expect, come from family firm or self-employed backgrounds. She identifies four particular categories.

There are those who have come to slip the bonds of the business. They have felt the pressure mounting on them and they have gone to take an MBA in order to avoid going back. It gives them an exit route.

Another group wants to acquire the skills that they cannot acquire just by doing the job. They want the abilities that will enable them to return in a safe and sensible way.

Others want to buy time. These people are still suffering a crisis of indecision. They know that if they return to the family business it is a commitment for life. They know the disappointment it may cause if they elect not to join the business. The MBA stays the evil hour – and, with luck, gives them another year of education with which to help them make a decision.

The last category are those who come with that decision-making in mind from the outset. They use their year to decide whether they want to join the family business and, if so, what the nature of the relationship with the business should be. Argument, discussion and study focus their minds on the issue.

Interestingly, one of Sue Birley's most popular seminars involves the family firm.

A case study for MBA students

In summary, the case study is this (Sue Birley, 1979, *The Small Business Casebook*):

R. J. Nevill is a small company which includes a printing business, a sub-post office and a retail shop. It was founded in 1785 but has always remained small. By 1976 it employed eighteen people and had a turnover of £87,523. During 1975 the owner died.

Despite a number of takeover offers, the family – Sheila (aged 49), Philip (21) and Vicky (19) – decided not to sell but to retain the family interest. They took this decision on the assumption that Philip would return to the business in 1977 when he had completed his degree. In the short term his mother, Sheila, would be managing director.

According to Philip, it was Sheila's position that caused them most thought when father died:

At 49, she was still relatively young and yet within the space of eighteen months her husband died and we had left home. We thought that the ideal solution for her future and for the business would be if she became an active managing director. This would provide her with an interest in life and it would solve the problem of management succession; from my own point of view, it would also enable me to complete my degree. However, although she did take over as sub-postmistress and although she did force herself to do some of the routine administration, she has never really taken to general management.

But now, as finals grow closer, I become less and less enthusiastic about my prospects. I know that not many people have such an opportunity handed to them but it isn't exactly an exciting business and it isn't as though I am being offered the chairmanship of ICI. What if I really don't like it? Will I be able to leave? What would I do then?

So what other considerations does Philip have to bear in mind? There is the tradition; the financial situation of his mother; and the roles of the employees and advisers. Says Philip:

The greatest strength of the company was the loyalty of the staff to the memory of my father, to his family and to the company. When my father died all the employees assumed, as I did, that I would step into his shoes. My continuing at university was a bit of a shock for them and morale has fallen to a very low ebb.

The issue is further complicated for me by Mum's position. At the very least she must have a reliable income to maintain, if not increase, her standard of living. I don't know much about running a business but I certainly know more than she does, even though she is doubtful about my capabilities at the moment. Actually, she is encouraged in this by John, our accountant, who although he is an old friend of my father's, has always disliked me. I think that he is jealous of me. This wouldn't matter if I felt that I could leave him to look after Mum's financial affairs but I am not sure even about that. The extent of his financial advice to her had been to keep all her money in the building society. As if she would ever need a mortgage! He has told her that as she is no longer going to work at Nevill's, she really shouldn't let them continue to pay for the telephone and the car. Apart from the rent from the lease of the property and my father's savings, her only income is the dividend from Nevill's.

Apart from Mum, there are five key personalities to consider.

Nancy, aged 54, is the manageress of the business. Her son also worked for us for a short while in 1969 but left to join the police. She has had a very close relationship with my father, an intimate knowledge of our customers, and generally has been the administrative mainstay since 1973. I know that she and her husband rely on the secure income and, along with the others, will draw a company pension when she retires at 60.

Ray, aged 50, is the sales representative. He has been with us since 1956 and has a very good reputation with the customers, providing the high quality of service they require. However, since the change in his salary structure in 1970 he has needed constant management and motivation. Since the death of my father his motivation has gradually waned to a level bordering on indifference.

Jenny, aged 53, is the chief cashier of the sub-post office. Although the post office was retained in the family name before and after 1974, Jenny has been the *de facto* sub-postmistress since about 1965; she is very efficient and trustworthy.

Bill, aged 54, is the foreman of the printing works. Although his knowledge of the printing methods is sound, he is very slow, uninspiring and prone to make many mistakes. The atmosphere in the printing works is depressing. Also, he has suffered from a weak heart since 1973.

John, aged 50, is the company accountant. He is the director of a local firm of accountants with whom he has been employed since leaving the local grammar school. My father used his services in the form of advice and over the years they became personal friends. Since 1975, he has taken on the roles of business adviser and family confidant. Unfortunately, during the settlement of my father's estate and the debate over the future of the business, I lacked credibility in the eyes of my mother and my sister. Although such phrases as 'of course it is up to you' were frequently used, the advice from him was valued far higher than anything I suggested. To do anything about this situation when I was not actually involved in the day-to-day running of the business was very difficult. It would have been impossible for me to replace him; firstly, I would not have received the necessary support from the family, and secondly because of his intimate knowledge of the business I needed him in the short term.

What do Philip's mother and sister think? Sheila recognises the short-term problems:

These last few years have been very disturbing for Philip and I know that he is having second thoughts about the business. That is only natural, but once he comes back home to his family and friends, I know that he will settle down very quickly.

He is very young to take on the responsibilities of a business but we do have a loyal and competent staff and John, our accountant, has promised to keep an eye on him. Meanwhile, I am giving him all the support that I can and trying not to show how worried I am.

As for Vicky, she does not believe that Philip should return. 'I think that we should just sell the business but Philip and Mum keep asking what the staff would do. Why can't they get another job?'

There were some sharp divisions among the Cranfield class as they discussed this scenario. What should Philip do? When it was taken to the vote, the majority voted for his selling R. J. Nevill to the management, despite the concern that they did not have either the skill or the motivation. Selling the business outright was the second most popular decision. Staying – and tackling the problems of the family firm – was third.

The class aroused passions. It aroused marked differences in opinion and approach. Afterwards, those students who represented a new generation of family firms were animated and persuasive in their views. There were flaws in the case study: it didn't deal with an autocratic father; it didn't deal with outside shareholders; it didn't deal with competitive siblings. But what animated them most was some recognition of problems that they themselves had experienced.

The first aspect of the case study that was discussed was the difference that can exist between generations. The goals, the interests and the education of Philip and his late father were at variance. His father had joined the company after the War and had stayed with the business since. Philip was at university – an opportunity denied to his father. His father had entered the business by a chance encounter while serving in the army; Philip had to decide whether to continue the business. Philip's aims and ambitions were greater than his father's.

Quite a few among this audience of graduates expressed sympathy for Philip; a few thought that it was a great opportunity (either to sell or to take it on).

Then the students discussed the pressures upon Philip. There was the pressure to provide income for his mother and also for his extended family, the workforce. There was the problem of the accountant. There was his father's ghost, laying expectations before him. There were his own ambitions, which potentially could be frustrated by the imposition of duty rather than being allowed to pursue a calling of his own choice. There was the problem that he, as a junior, would have in leading and managing elders.

It was identified that if he returned to the family firm, he would in the first instance merely be climbing into his father's shoes and carrying on. The possibility of changing things at the company would be circumscribed by an unwritten contract and by the perceptions of his inexperience. Was Philip credible enough?

What were the problems that he faced? There was the credibility with his mother, who patently was unsure of him. There was the accountant, who had become a personal family friend rather than being a trained adviser. There was his own self-doubt.

The students then outlined the options that the company faced. Philip could sell to the managers, because they had the experience and worked as a team. Of course, there was the question of whether, as a tripartite business, it should be split and sold or sold as one. Disposal to the extended family, or at least a split between ownership and management, found the greatest favour among the audience.

If the company was to be sold outright, there were clearly tax implications and the looming problem of Sheila's future income which might not be enough. And who would buy it? Where would they find a purchaser? Was John, the accountant, the right man to provide the network of potential purchasers?

Another option that was proposed was to bring in an outside manager. But the type of manager that the company could attract was not an inspiring one – preferably old, cheap, an accountant, and a person who would only be interested in keeping things ticking over. It was decided that this was not the dynamic character that the company required.

As noted the audience voted for a sale of the company. And, in reality, that was what Philip did do.

Where does this case study and anecdote fit into education and training? The response to the case study was an interested one. The discussion centred on family matters rather than strategic business plans and it provoked a wide range of reactions. The thirst for discussion was apparent.

This is confirmed by Sue Birley herself:

Those who go to Cranfield already have one degree which in itself
represented one break with the firm. Some will have worked in the
family firms; others will have trained as accountants or in multinational
companies. But the experience that they will have had has some link
back to the family firm.

And they come to Cranfield with emotional and intellectual baggage.
Some may arrive with the family business in a mess and feel responsibility towards it. And that responsibility has not been imposed by their
parents; it has been self-imposed.

They arrive with an understanding of self-employment. They arrive
with an understanding of cash flow and of customer relationships in
their bones.

When these students come to Cranfield, though, they learn
other things that enable them to put the family business into
a broader perspective. They learn about business as an entity –
not as a symbol. While their parents might have been driven by a
fascination for a product or a set of products, these inheritors are
being driven by strategic matters, by the business as a business.
They learn that there are no set rules, contrary to what many
fathers might have told them, but only a matrix of skills, emotions
and situations that they will each confront and shape in their
particular manner.

The potential conflicts

It may strike many as being uncomfortable and disturbing. A
parent runs a business and earns a good living from it, enough
to pay for their children to go to university and maybe also
to business school (although many would say that the children
themselves should pay for this last stage of education). Having
been to business school, in order (so the parent thinks) for them
to come back into the fold and take over the business, the children
actually come back with schemes of closure, disposal or sale
as high on their list of possible ideas as talk of growth and
development. Surely that isn't what they should be teaching at
business school?

The answer is, of course, 'of course it is'. The question that
should be addressed is: 'What makes the inheritor interested?'
On the part of the parent, that entails an understanding of the
new culture, the new attitudes that are prevalent, and adjust-
ing accordingly. It also requires a sympathy and understanding

among the new generation – and that sympathy can get lost in the confidence that surrounds someone once they have the magic letters MBA after their name.

So far, I have not come across a family firm where the value of an MBA has been disputed by those who have obtained one. Clive Cutler, managing director of Pearce & Cutler, is quite categorical on the value of his Ashridge MBA. He is also rigidly honest in his assessment of himself beforehand:

Neither my brother or I had the edges rubbed off us. It had been a long-protected business. We had a protection around us that we would not have had outside. I very much regret that I didn't put my foot down harder. I didn't want to come into the business but my father was unwell so I came in straight away. I wanted to widen my experience, although entering the family business had been a long-term idea. What I had thought of doing was spending at least three years gaining an industrial experience. I wanted – no, I needed – to be a management accountant and I had to obtain that outside the family firm and not even necessarily in the same trade. I succumbed to a certain degree of pressure even though inside the family business I learned a bit about the glazing processes. I spent a year learning the trade – and I had never had any other form of training.

Ashridge was my next stage. I wanted to break away, widen my experience and help break some of the emotional ties by having a manager manage this business while I was away. It was an experience which I hope will enable me to deal with things slightly differently. I could deal with institutions differently and certainly better than the first time when I was green and rather at their beck and call. There was a stage when I did not know enough to disagree, when I was not sure that the best interests of the business were being served. I allowed others to dictate while I wanted to be in the driving seat.

Ashridge fulfilled those expectations. It gave me a distance when I could have got too close to the family business. I am now setting in motion a strategic plan that will change the business fundamentally.

Naturally, much of this can be ascribed to the differences that exist between generations. However, now that management education has embedded its roots into the business culture, the difference will be greater than ever before. The potential managing director, studying and learning with a far wider range of people than father ever did, is going to have markedly different perspectives. The cosiness of the family firm may be foregone for a dynamic growth company or for an international career. In other words, the family firm has to compete against a more demanding set of expectations.

The balance between tradition and modern management

Now there are two aspects to this challenge. The family business must show itself to be capable of change, to be an attractive business in which personal development – of a level anticipated in some large corporations or small, high-powered firms – can be achieved. But it must also stay true to its principles, to the family vision, from which it can derive a unique strength that few non-family firms can match.

'Falling into the business' is no longer going to be acceptable. It should not be acceptable to the parents, who have to set strict criteria for including their children. It should not be acceptable to the children, who must see the true potential of their parents' business before they embark on a lifetime of commitment. But once this has been done, a clear course of development needs to be set out, with mutually understood objectives.

For prospective managers and directors of the organisation, the lessons of Professor Charles Handy's *The Making of Managers* (1988) are even more important. Handy found that over one-third of British managers had had no management training since they started work and only one-fifth had degrees or professional qualifications of any kind. The British were well outstripped by the West Germans and the Americans. These findings have been backed up by other studies and research projects. Accident and chance, unstructured and unorganised – these are the criteria by which many managers have been trained. It is not hard to see that many family businesses could fall into this category.

Training by responsibility

On the other hand, it could be argued that the cloak of responsibility that beckons so many family members is in itself a kind of training. This is well put by Bob Garratt in his book *The Learning Organisation* (1987):

Matters were easier for the old-established 'dynastic' family firms because the people who rose to the top had been socialized from birth to the kind of thinking necessary to retain and nurture the family 'heritage'. With the growth of modern corporations, shareholders and their agents (the managers) have been separated and the socialization process has been lost.

Yet, as Garratt goes on to demonstrate, directors in so many of the companies that he has studied 'do not give direction, do not monitor changes in the social, economic and political environment in which they exist, and so do not ensure the survival of their organisations by being able to adapt their organisations to the rate of change in those environments.' Which is precisely why so many family firms have failed or have been overtaken by events.

So family members come into contact with the business at an early age. They come into contact with a business that has many flaws – although they are not necessarily seen from the perspective of the living room and kitchen at home – which could impede the learning and training of potential successors. The distance which has to be created, and which many will find near-impossible, is one which enables the young to look at the entirety of the company. This does not come from what the Americans occasionally refer to as 'dinner table training'.

A balance has to be found between the inculcation of values, the stimulating of enthusiasm and the need to recognise potential competence. Fathers have to instil a desire and a pride about the business; they also have to be clear-sighted as to whether the son or daughter is competent enough to take it up. The lurking danger is that the capable heir then decides that they do not want to go back. But if that risk is not taken, then the possibility for nepotism and incompetence is increased. You don't necessarily need your children to get a first class degree at Oxford followed by an MBA at Harvard, but you do need a sign.

Then there must be a time of learning. Many heads of family businesses have said to me that they would rather have done something else before entering the family business. Circumstances may dictate otherwise, but it seems incumbent upon the parent to encourage the future successor to travel, to work in other companies, in other words to learn.

After that, there is the training path. Even in the smallest company, heirs must work their way up and prove themselves at every different stage. Here the danger is in setting the heir artificially high standards, in expecting far greater performance and productivity than of others.

A mentor for the heir

At this stage, it is also worth considering an adviser or mentor for the putative heir. Coming up through the organisation, with the weight of public and private expectation on your shoulders, can be a daunting experience. It requires a confidant who also understands the business and its culture. Instruction, wisdom and a shoulder to cry on – if you can identify such a figure in your company, use them.

In one company that I studied, the managing director, Ian Dixon, was officially an outsider. He had joined the long-established family firm of John Willmott and had worked his way to the top, becoming managing director while a member of the family, Peter Willmott, was chairman. When Ian Dixon joined the company, Peter's 95-year-old father was still managing director. Peter trained in a variety of jobs but when his father had to be succeeded the job was passed to one John Budgen. 'Peter had recognised that perhaps he wasn't right to run a building company and he identified that it was in the firm's best interests to have an external person to run it', says Ian. Then Peter became chairman and Ian took over from John Budgen. It was a great day for Ian – he had always wanted to run a building company but ownership up to that time had not interested him.

'Peter and I work back to back', he says. 'He has an external role. It's one that only he could play because he has the name.' The arrangement worked well but there was a limit to it – Ian's ambitions, having reached a certain stage, needed something extra. And so Willmott became Willmott Dixon, a two-family business after 135 years.

'I'm very grateful', says Dixon. 'I was allowed to come in and run his company. All the details are left to me. And an owner who doesn't interfere is rare, I think. We have watched many others where the sons have come along and then gone bust because that next generation was wrong. In family businesses you can be blind to the potential ineptitudes.'

Dixon admits to a degree of hesitancy about the suggestion of his joining as an owner. The Willmotts were, after all, the trustees of a five generation firm. He quotes a letter from one major company: 'I would not be truthful if I didn't say that I was surprised that a company should change its name after 135 years – if the reasons justify the change?' But, says Dixon, 'I was delighted and surprised at the change.'

One of the strengths that this has brought to the company is the way that a successor can now be groomed, with Dixon acting as a trainer and monitor.

We took John Willmott through the group with a strong reporting system to evaluate where he fitted best. Richard Willmott wanted to be a site manager so he is going through a five-year programme and I plan his development so that I am in a good position to evaluate it.

There are differences in the development programme for the young Willmotts. Firstly, Dixon does it. The only others he follows are senior management. Secondly, he says:

It would be wrong not to recognise that in the last analysis I could sack senior management. The sons won't go so the job is to find them a niche. You have to recognise that they have a burden too. The greatest problem is not my attitude or theirs but that of the staff. They cannot be evaluated properly if they are treated differently and I know that the staff found it very difficult to accept that they were not just ordinary trainees.

This points again to the necessity of outside training and experience for the new generation of the family firm. Without it, the probability of introversion and eventual decline becomes greater, particularly in the light of enhanced competition from overseas competitors. Not only do such competitors attack from a strong financial base, they attack from a strong and broad base of knowledge. If the tough and skilful are the ones who will survive, then the family firm needs to ask itself some key questions. What will be required to survive in this market-place? To what extent have we those qualities, either within the family or within our workforce? What steps can we take to arm family members with those abilities and what steps do we need to take to develop them in our employees?

The Mercedes Benz training course

In 1985, Mercedes Benz was approaching its centennial and a keynote speech had to be prepared for the grand dealer convention and dinner. At the same time some dealer-principals had been saying that they regretted the absence of a training programme for their sons and daughters. The chief executive decided that there should be one, particularly as this demand coincided with the loss of a number of dealerships – they were being tempted by attractive offers from large groups whose finances were being buoyed up by a bull stock market. According to the company's personnel director, Peter Padley, there was a target audience of some forty to fifty young people.

There were other objectives: to attract young people who had grown up in the shadow of their father, who was probably both entrepreneurial and wealthy, into the motor trade when their personal circumstances might have made them wish to escape. The other objective was succession. As Padley puts it:

An entrepreneurial father running a successful business, and enjoying running that successful business, traditionally doesn't talk to his children about handing it over. Now we did not want to talk to the fathers about this but we wanted to establish a mechanism that would bring it to the surface at a later stage.

Mercedes decided that a solid course of a number of consecutive weeks was not practical, although the need for an extensive and varied training lasting six weeks was identified.

Regional managers were asked to select potential candidates. The next step was to devise a course that would prove to be attractive to the candidates and that would appear worthwhile to the parents – and which would justify the £5,000 that they were going to be charged. The regional managers thought that nobody would come – but come they did.

Then Padley talked to the business schools. The prospect of Harvard was a good one for the price tag. Professor Louis Barnes was asked to participate; not only would he run the week's course at Harvard and examine the total content of the course, he would also meet with the parents beforehand to ask them what they thought and would then meet them afterwards to address with them the question of succession.

We hoped that at the meeting some parents would say to other parents, 'you really have to let go of the business' and 'you have to come to some sort of plan with your children, otherwise they will lose interest and drift away.' And that's exactly what happened. It worked extremely well.

The six weeks were divided into three fortnights. The first two were spent at the UK headquarters at Milton Keynes; the second two in Germany; and the last two in the United States. Each of the first four weeks was themed: one week studied leadership, another would study computer and business skills. Books – such as the Iacocca best-seller – were read, presentations had to be made, speakers came to talk on political or environmental matters. The atmosphere was a competitive one, with individuals or teams working against each other.

Week five was run in Boston by two Harvard professors. This, says Padley, was the most testing week. A series of case studies was used to bring out all the issues facing family businesses. 'A lot of them were about issues that had been discussed formally out of class time', says Padley. 'Suddenly they found that they were extremely eager to talk to each other about these issues. Who holds the shares? What happens when father hands over? What if a sibling wants to come back into the business? The case study exercise was really quite difficult for them. They didn't appreciate just how deeply a tutor can go into it, teasing out all the problems.'

In the final week the candidates were sent to visit car and truck dealers in various parts of the United States. 'It was important that they saw how the world's biggest automotive market works.'

Mercedes is pleased with the results. The ultimate test of such a course was whether the family business stayed with the franchise, and Padley received a lot of feedback from the parents:

There is plenty of anecdotal evidence that it was successful, but we have not measured it qualitatively and I don't know whether we would. What we do know is that parents almost unanimously believe that there has been a quantum change in their sons and daughters.

We know how many are still in the business and that the support networks are working strongly. For example, one of the most difficult aspects of the car business is the development of used cars as an activity. The groups who went on the courses swap notes with each other almost on a daily basis about used cars – and they trade with each other. We have probably lost three or four dealerships. But at a launch in Spain I found myself on a table with six of the guys from the first course. I think that's a manifestation about what a family business can mean.

It was not an easy task assembling such a course. Padley encountered many doubting Thomases. He was also realistic about the possible weaknesses of his candidates.

We were dealing with young people who may have grown up with all the money that they really need. So perhaps there was not the discipline. They may be slightly spoiled. Six weeks of fairly stretching work was quite a challenge.

They had to prove that they had the skills. They had to be able to address the question: 'Why the hell should you take charge of 100 people simply because you are the son or daughter of your father?' If they were going to be the custodians of others' livelihoods and welfare then they have to know something about running a business.

There were some parents who disagreed with our objectives. One father told me: 'I think that the most able person in the business at a particular point in time should take over from me.' Yet his four children, all of whom were working for other companies, were just the types of people that we were wanting to attract back to Mercedes. Others were equally straightforward, expressing the view that it should not be a God-given right for someone to take over what may be a multi-million pound business just because of blood.

There were also a number of senior managers in large dealerships who thought that the whole idea was really rather twee and probably not serious enough. On the other hand, quite a few wanted to join the course!

But as far as Padley is concerned, the main vote of confidence came from the fathers, who supported their children with the money and the time off work.

The father has made a lot of brave decisions over the past twenty years and has taken a lot of risks. He has also made a lot of money. More than anything in his life he wants to hand that business on. The starting-point is that he hopes his children will want to follow him into the business – and if the children are normal, they probably don't. That's why fathers found this course attractive. If it could make the auto industry attractive, then it would help him to bridge the gap. Before, the father was pursuing this wish and the normal chemistry was at work; the son could not wait for the day when he could get away from his father and father was extremely disappointed at this lack of interest. Often the business would be sold, almost as a gesture. I think that this course has succeeded in this area but we have not completely cracked this question of 'How does a father hand the business over?' There is only one thing that does work and that is death. Once he feels he is ready to hand it over, he is saying to himself, 'Now is the time to die'. There has only been one father who decided to hand over in his mid-fifties and back out – and that has been extremely successful.

Bibliography

Barnes, Louis and Hershon, Simon (1976) 'Transferring power in the family business', *Harvard Business Review*, July–August.

Barnet, Correlli (1986) *The Audit of War*, Macmillan.

Barry, Bernard (1975) 'The development of organisation structure in the family firm', *Journal of General Management*, 3 (1).

Birley, Sue (1979) The Small Business Casebook, Macmillan, London.

Birley, Sue (1986) 'Succession in the family firm: the inheritor's view', *Journal of Small Business Management*, July.

Bracewell-Milnes, Barry (1989) 'The wealth of giving everyone his inheritance', Institute of Economic Affairs.

Burns, Paul and Dewhurst, Jim (1989) *Small Business and Entrepreneurship*, Macmillan.

Clutterbuck, David and Crainer, Stuart (1988) *The Decline and Rise of British Industry*, Mercury.

Donnelley, Robert (1964) 'The family business', *Harvard Business Review*, July–August.

Dyer, W. Gibb (1986) *Cultural Change in Family Firms*, Jossey-Bass.

Garratt, Robert (1987) *The Learning Organisation*, Fontana/Collins.

Halberstam, David (1987) *The Reckoning*, Bloomsbury.

Handy, Charles (1988) *The Making of Managers*, Pitman.

Hayward, Stoy (1989) 'Staying the course: survival characteristics of the family owned business', produced in conjunction with the London Business School, July.

Levinson, Harry (1971) 'Conflicts that plague family businesses', *Harvard Business Review*, March–April.

McWhinney, Will 'Therapist to family business', *New Management*.

Metzger, Robert (1988) 'Guidelines for tomorrow's consultants', *Journal of Management Consulting*, 4 (4).

Pearson, Barrie (1989) *Successful Acquisition of Unquoted Companies*, Gower.

Poe, Randan (1980) 'The SOBs', *The Conference Board*, May.

Sampson, Anthony (1971) *The New Anatomy of Britain*, Hodder and Stoughton

Saunders, James (1989), *Nightmare*, Hutchinson, London.

Stillerman, Barry (1989), *Inheritance Tax: A practical guide*, 2nd edn, Stoy Hayward.

Ziegler, Philip (1988) *The Sixth Great Power: Barings, 1762–1929*, Collins.

Index